Revenue Management in Service Organizations

Revenue Management in Service Organizations

Paul Rouse
University of Auckland, New Zealand

William Maguire
University of Tasmania, Australia

Julie Harrison
University of Auckland, New Zealand

Revenue Management in Service Organizations

First published in 2010 by
Business Expert Press, LLC
222 East 46th Street, New York, NY 10017
www.businessexpertpress.com

ISBN-13: 978-1-60649-147-8 (paperback)

ISBN-13: 978-1-60649-148-5 (e-book)

10.4128/ 9781606491485

A publication in the Business Expert Press Managerial Accounting collection

Collection ISSN: 2152-7113 (print)
Collection ISSN: 2152-7121 (electronic)

Cover design by Jonathan Pennell
Interior design by Scribe, Inc.

First edition: January 2011

10 9 8 7 6 5 4 3 2 1

Printed in Taiwan

Abstract

Revenue management is concerned with maximizing revenue flows while controlling costs. This is a new management framework combining conventional management accounting concepts and methods with notions of yield management, pricing, and process management. The revenue objective provides a unifying goal for the aforementioned concepts and methods that are especially suitable for service organizations, where revenue considerations are inextricably linked to the activities performed. While our focus is on service organizations, any organization will find something of value in this book.

For chief financial officers, this book places revenue management at the forefront of accounting, with cost management and performance measurement in supporting roles. Revenue management introduces new ideas, such as yield management, while uniting previously disparate subjects such as project management, capacity costing, and the theory of constraints. Methods of pricing and their associated strategies are included as well as techniques for segmenting consumer markets.

Our focus is predominantly on service organizations, such as airlines, hotels, restaurants, and cinemas, as well as professional service firms, such as auditors, lawyers, and architects. Most service organizations differ from traditional manufacturing in that services cannot usually be stored as inventory. These organizations are critically dependent on the quality of service delivery. In fact, any organization that has service as a key part of its value strategy will benefit from a systematic understanding of revenue management.

Our book will introduce the reader to some of the more important methods, such as yield management, using simple examples as well as providing practical guidelines to pricing and process management. While we include conventional management accounting concepts and techniques, our emphasis is on the use of these techniques in revenue management, encompassing a focus on revenue drivers as well as cost drivers. We also use several well-established techniques, with new applications, such as the use of critical path analysis to model restaurant processes and key bottlenecks.

Keywords

Revenue management, service organizations, yield management, pricing, process management

Contents

Preface

Millions of people experience revenue management every day, but you will search in vain to find courses on revenue management in most universities and business schools. The subject does encompass a large number of subject areas, which might explain why it does not feature as a subject in its own right. Furthermore, some of the methods involve sophisticated mathematics and statistics, which many business school students tend to avoid. We hope that this book will stimulate interest in this neglected area and fill a major gap in business school education.

For our part, we have researched and taught revenue management as part of our undergraduate and postgraduate courses for over 7 years. As part of our teaching, we have prepared a substantial volume of case studies, exercises, and examples of revenue management in practice. Some of that material appears in this book to support our goal of spreading the word about revenue management.

The focus on service organizations reflects this sector's growing importance in most economies. The *OECD Observer*[1] reports that the services sector now accounts for over 70% of total employment and value-added in Organization for Economic Co-operation and Development (OECD) countries. It also accounts for almost all employment growth.[2] Consequently, the main emphasis of this book is on services, but the lessons are equally applicable to manufacturing organizations.

Over the years, we have supervised many postgraduate students who have studied revenue management practices in restaurants, car rental firms, cinemas, airlines, and, more recently, in small- to medium-sized firms. We have published articles on revenue management and other related articles on performance measurement. Our current research continues with creating product groupings in traditional service areas (e.g., home care for the elderly), pricing behavior in networks, and the relationship between economic performance and sustainability.

We hope our background and experience in delivering education specifically in revenue management has helped us to produce a user-friendly book for broader consumption. We hope that you find it so and that it will stimulate you to pursue this exciting area.

We would like to acknowledge the assistance of colleagues and friends in developing our material over the years, including Jennifer Kerr, Ralph Kober, and Garrett van Ryzin. We would also like to thank Ken Merchant for his insightful comments in editing this book.

CHAPTER 1

Revenue Management

An Overview

Introduction

Revenue management provides organizations with new opportunities to improve their profitability and cash flows. It does this through a combination of sophisticated methods and more refined ways of examining organization processes. We will explain and illustrate these in this book where the focus is on transferring knowledge about revenue management to managers who wish to implement them in practice. Although revenue management is relatively new, whether we know it or not, we encounter revenue management practices almost every day. Consider the following scenarios.

1. A two-star hotel with 120 rooms has two rates: a high rate of $200 per night and a discount rate of $110 per night. Ideally, management would like to have all rooms occupied at $200 per night (the full rate), but this may not be achievable. Assume that the reservations manager receives a booking request 1 month in advance for a room at the discount rate of $110. Should she accept the booking at the lower rate or wait, in the hope that a booking at a higher rate will eventuate? If she rejects the booking, the room may remain unoccupied. If she accepts the booking, the hotel may have to turn down a booking at the higher rate.
2. A popular restaurant is always full in peak periods but makes only mediocre returns. Food costs appear to be excessively high and although waiting times for customers are extensive in peak times,

the restaurant is usually well below 50% occupancy in the remaining opening times.

3. An accounting firm struggles to meet deadlines and to provide speedy turnaround responses to its clients. Delays are common, and clients are increasingly upset over the service the firm provides. In response, the firm argues that all clients are treated equally and delays are due to increased compliance requirements imposed by the government.

All three scenarios contain opportunities for improvement through revenue management. The chapters in this book describe how you can achieve this. Airlines, hotels, amusement parks, restaurants, and golf courses are just some of the organizations that have made substantial gains in profitability through practicing revenue management. Former American Airlines chairman and CEO Robert Crandall described revenue management as the most important technical development in transportation management since deregulation of the airlines. Many organizations practicing revenue management claim to have increased revenues substantially. A recent story about pricing baseball tickets like airline seats in *BusinessWeek*[1] quotes the San Francisco Giants' ticketing chief as stating that the adoption of a new revenue technology could add $5 million or more to the revenue for 2010.

Revenue management aims to improve an organization's performance by obtaining the best revenue streams possible from its resources. This involves balancing revenue initiatives with managing processes and resources. There is little point in improving one process if this is outweighed by the deterioration of others. Virtually any organization can profit from revenue management.[2] In this book, we show you how to apply new techniques and insights that provide the opportunity to improve revenue flows while controlling costs and investment.

It is not just about maximizing revenue but also about managing resources and related costs of both usage and investment. Figure 1.1 shows a broad picture of the key components that we address in this book. We shall use the three scenarios to illustrate these components.

The first scenario relates to the price and yield components on the right-hand side of Figure 1.1. In turn, these involve the factors in the box. Since there are two prices or rates for the same room, the hotel has segmented

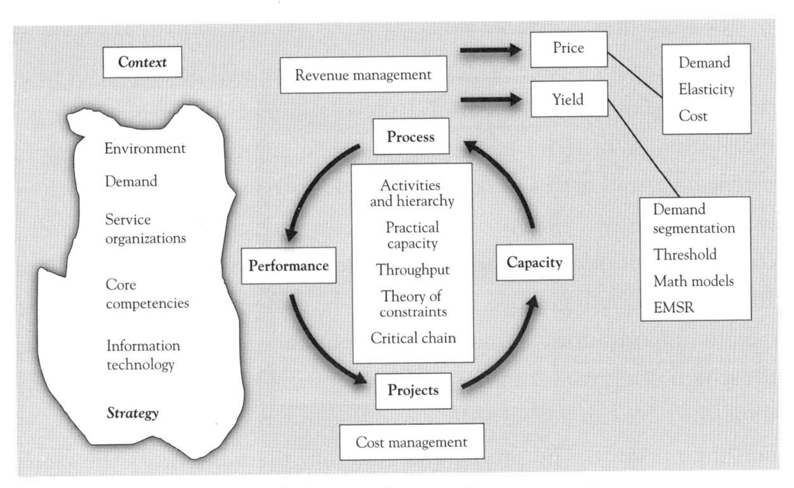

Figure 1.1. Attributes of the supplier product or service

its customers into two types: those who are price sensitive and those who are not. By introducing different requirements for each (e.g., to obtain a discounted price, the room must be booked at least 3 weeks in advance), the hotel has created two separate products in the minds of its customers even though the room itself remains unchanged. Ideally, the hotel would like to rent all its rooms at the higher price, but this is unlikely. Consider two extremes: if the hotel refuses to rent any discounted rooms, it is likely to end up with unoccupied rooms. This means lost revenue. If it rents all its rooms at the discounted price in advance, there will inevitably be some customers who would have been willing to pay the higher price closer to the night of stay but who are now lost sales because there are no rooms available. The solution is obviously between these extremes and requires balancing a certain sale now at the discounted price with a less-certain sale at the high price closer to the night of the stay. This sounds like the old adage "a bird in the hand is worth two in the bush," and the methods for dealing with this include the threshold method and some mathematical models. Of the mathematical models, the two that we will describe and explain are expected marginal seat revenue (EMSR), which is the common method used by airlines and hotels, and linear programming. Any organization is able to use any of the models, but this will require information about demand forecasts and segmenting its customer demand into multiple products.

We have all probably experienced the second scenario in the form of either waiting for a table or deliberately choosing to dine outside of peak times to avoid the rush. Figure 1.1 shows a number of revenue management options. In terms of pricing and yield approaches, we can try to manage demand across peak and off-peak periods using devices such as early-bird specials, two-for-one dining, free entertainment, or even discounted menu prices. These methods are visible to customers but need additional marketing efforts if they are to be effective. An alternative is to look for opportunities to improve the restaurant's processes. For example, the length of time or duration a table is occupied determines how many times the table can be "turned" (i.e., different sets of diners within a certain time period). The shorter the duration, the more times the tables turn, and the greater the number of customers the restaurant can serve. But customers may not like to feel that they are being hurried during their meal, particularly if they are in a restaurant that they have chosen to celebrate a special occasion. The strategy of the restaurant determines the actions taken. If a restaurant has positioned itself as an exclusive location specializing in fine dining, then its best action is to use pricing to manage peak and off-peak demand. However, even in this situation, there are some actions that the restaurant can take to manage duration. For a restaurant that is medium-priced and caters to diners who want to eat in a pleasant environment but who are less concerned about the specialness of the occasion, a number of options for managing duration are available. Examples include streamlining the menu in peak times, training the waiting staff to avoid suggestive selling during peak times, and "guiding" customers into menu selections that can be more easily filled by the kitchen, thereby reducing preparation time. The secret to duration management is to reduce time spent on activities that are not perceived as adding value to the customers, such as waiting time between servings.

While most of us would recognize the first two scenarios, we do not experience the third scenario quite so often, as we tend to use professional firms less frequently than restaurants or hotels. Nonetheless, many professional organizations experience these problems, and Figure 1.1 shows some of the ways in which revenue management can provide solutions. The mention of deadlines invokes comparison with construction projects, and service organizations can use the same management principles and methods as those used in project management. Furthermore, the major task facing any service business is managing its capacity and capabilities. The theory of constraints, discussed in Chapter 4, uses the idea of a bottleneck to focus on improving its throughput (the rate at which clients are processed and revenue is earned). A bottleneck is the resource or process whose capacity is the primary restriction on how fast volumes can be produced or processed. Often, the bottleneck is a person who authorizes the work or provides a specialization or skill that every job must go through. Mapping the processes and the sequence of these processes can identify bottlenecks as well as reveal potential areas for improvement.

We refer to Figure 1.1 throughout this chapter and the remainder of this book. The important message at this stage is that although revenue management covers many areas, we can boil them down to those that are externally based or visible to the outside world (pricing and yield management) and those that are internally based and not so visible (processes, performance, cost management, and capacity). Revenue management is an all-encompassing approach to the management of the revenue, expenses, and investment areas of an organization. In some ways, it is an old idea repackaged into powerful concepts and techniques that can dramatically improve an organization's financial performance.

On the subject of old ideas, two centuries ago in 1849, Dupuit wrote on the subject of trains:

> It is not because of the few thousand francs which would have to be spent to put a roof over the third-class carriages or to upholster the third-class seats that some company or other has open carriages with wooden benches. What the company is trying to do is prevent the passengers who can pay the second-class fare from travelling third-class; it hits the poor, not because it wants to hurt them, but to frighten the rich[3] (quoted by Ekelund).[4]

This book focuses on the items displayed in Figure 1.1 and explains them using nontechnical language as much as possible. We occasionally resort to more technical terms when this is unavoidable and accompany them with suitable explanations for the benefit of the reader. We also try to minimize technical calculations by putting these inside a sidebar that we have labeled, "*Where does the number come from?*" You, the reader, can ignore these sidebars without interrupting the flow of the discussion.

This book does not cover all areas. It is not a book about finance or marketing, and although we discuss costing systems, it is not a book about accounting, either. Although information systems are a key feature of many revenue management systems (think airlines), we do not describe these. Similarly, we do not describe sophisticated methods of yield management involving complex mathematical programming and statistical methods. We aim to acquaint the reader with the basic ideas behind revenue management and to provide references for those wishing to pursue the topic in more depth. We also envisage that many managers do not want to understand all the technical details but do want to have a broad understanding of how it works in order to be able to converse with the technical experts. In the chapters that follow, we provide numerous examples in describing the technical material but maintain a high-level perspective on where this material fits into revenue management. If you get lost, come back to Figure 1.1, which shows the main areas of revenue management within an organization. We explicitly include contextual factors in the organization's structure, strategy, and environment, as these affect the implementation and operation of revenue management. The other main areas include price and yield, process, projects, performance, and capacity. While these may appear to be distinct, Figure 1.1 depicts significant flows among them. This is the nature of real-life systems, which makes them interesting phenomena to study. It also provides a holistic view of how organizations function and enables us to show how techniques within each area interact and complement each other. We briefly describe each of these areas and refer to the relevant chapter that explains them in greater detail. Before doing this, we explain "willingness to pay," a fundamental concept that we regularly refer to throughout this book.

Willingness to Pay

Willingness to pay is a key concept in pricing and yield management, and it underpins many of the issues surrounding value and nonvalue adding that are discussed in later chapters. As the expression suggests, customers vary in how much money they are willing to pay for a product or service. Some customers are willing to pay a high price, while others will purchase only at a lower price. This reflects, to a large extent, the relative value they are placing on a product or service that embodies their perception of the product or service. The diagram in Figure 1.2 represents the features or attributes of a product or service from a supplier perspective. The circle titled "supplier" contains a series of dots that represent product or service attributes, for example, technical features of the product itself, such as functionality, ease of use, reliability, and fit for the job; aesthetic features such as appearance, feel, and attractiveness; and support features such as service, parts, and warranties. These are all attributes that the supplier believes customers value or think that the product or service should contain.

The number of attributes or dots can vary from product to product, although Chapter 3 describes how the same underlying product can be differentiated into many products. Since the supplier knows their product inside and out, they are usually aware of all the bells and whistles that are provided. Suppliers therefore tend to see their products or services differently than customers.

Figure 1.3 shows the interaction of two clients with the supplier and reveals two related dimensions of willingness to pay: (a) clients who do not want all the bells and whistles a supplier provides and (b) clients who value all the supplier product attributes differently.

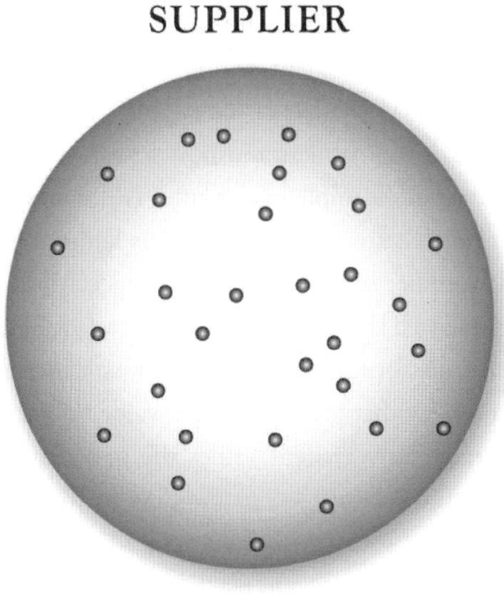

SUPPLIER

Figure 1.2. Supplier's perception of features or attributes of their product or service

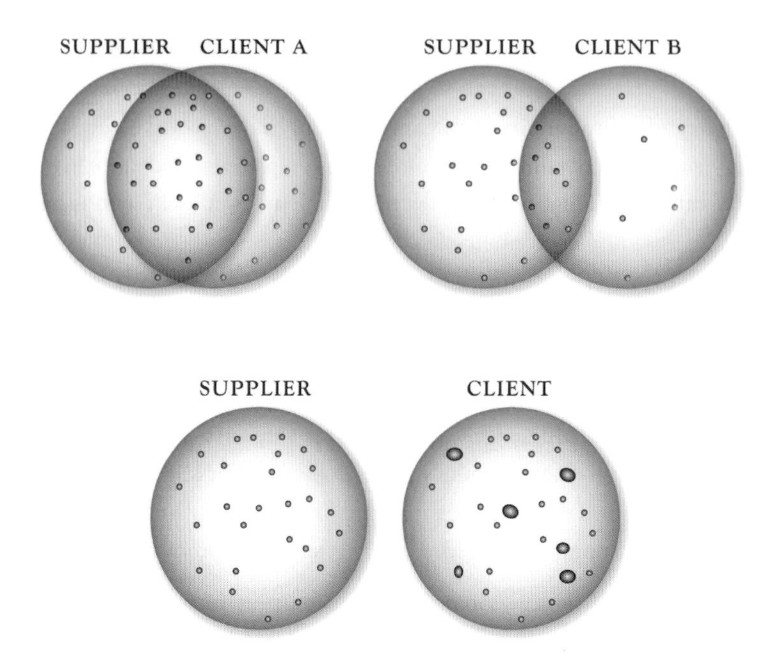

Figure 1.3. Willingness to pay as a marriage between supplier and client: **Panel A: Clients only want particular attributes and not others. Panel B: A client has varying values for the supplier's product attributes.**

In Panel A, two clients are depicted by two respective circles, and these overlap the supplier's circle. Client A likes many of the attributes provided by the supplier. In contrast, client B only wants some of them. There remain some attributes (to the left of the supplier circle) that both clients either do not want, do not understand how to use, or of which they are simply ignorant. A good example of the latter is the many features found in software packages that are available, but users fail to use them. It is also apparent that the supplier fails to meet all the expectations or needs of clients A and B, represented by the area on the right of the circles. These areas provide an opportunity for the supplier to work with the client to *co-create* a new product or service that provides greater value to both parties.

Panel B illustrates how a client values the product attributes differently, as shown by the relative size of the dots in the right-hand circle. The larger the dot, the greater the value placed on that attribute. The smaller the dot, the lower the value placed on the attribute. Some attributes are not valued at all, and a careful comparison will reveal where a dot that appears in the supplier's circle does not appear in the client's circle. Different clients can have different values for the product attributes. In fact, Panel B can be seen as underpinning the difference in clients' use of a product's attributes, which stems from differences in the value placed on these.

Willingness to pay is a common theme throughout this book, and we provide numerous examples to illustrate this more clearly. Next, we briefly describe the major features of Figure 1.1 and where these features appear in each chapter.

Context (Chapter 2)

We are all most likely familiar with the three most important things to look for when purchasing a house: "location, location, location." In shaping appropriate strategies, refer to "context, context, context" as the three most important things. Strategy essentially refers to the relationship between the organization and its environment. To be successful, it must understand both the environment in which it operates and the characteristics, such as consumer demand, that have special relevance in this context. The human factor is a key factor, especially in service organizations, and core competencies form an important input into strategy, as they not only determine an organization's ability to react to changes in its business environment but also affect how well it manages its capacity and capabilities. Likewise, information technology continually offers opportunities for improving existing revenue or for finding new ways of earning revenue, and it also facilitates efficiency and effectiveness in cost management. Last, but not least, is the notion that every organization is a service organization. Gone are the days when product was the sole output; nowadays, every organization is concerned with how its output is received by consumers, and, increasingly, the service dimension is the dominant feature. This focus on services has even been named "service science" by IBM, and revenue management can be viewed as part of this.

The way that an organization tackles its environment is its strategy. This determines how it prices and organizes its internal processes. In fact, we will see that yield management is a strategy in its own right, as it requires that you both identify and segment the market in which you decide to operate. Chapter 2 describes some established approaches to strategy, some of which may already be familiar to you, such as cost leadership and differentiation. For example, pricing decisions will differ for a cost leadership strategy (aiming to price below the market average) when compared to a differentiation strategy (aiming to price above the market average).

Pricing and Yield (Chapter 3)

Demand-based pricing seeks to extract the optimum amount from the market given the demand conditions. The ability to stimulate and manage demand requires knowledge of the market, including how customers respond to changes in price (known as price elasticity of demand). For example, if an airline drops its airfares, will that attract additional customers or will it merely retain existing customers who are paying less than they would have been prepared to pay? The key is consumers' *willingness to pay*, which underlies demand-based pricing and leads us to an important lesson: *not all consumers have the same willingness to pay!*

Panels A and B in Figure 1.3 illustrate differences in the marriage between client needs and the attributes supplied and also provide an explanation for why demand curves in economics are usually depicted as downward sloping, where high price levels have lower demand than lower price levels. Although Panel A does not show the utility placed by each client on attributes, it does provide an insight as to why client A may have greater willingness to pay than client B. In short, client B does not want the same product as client A, and this is where yield management comes into play, because we can then have different prices or rates for the same product or service. After all, a seat on a plane or a room in a hotel is the same product or service, but differences in customers' willingness to pay allow us to charge different prices. Chapter 3 examines the next question, which is how to decide how many seats or room nights to allocate to each price or rate class. In other words, the issue becomes how to manage the product mix to extract the maximum revenue, which is what we call yield management. Chapter 3 describes some commonly used yield management methods: threshold curves, EMSR model, and linear programming.

While yield management works well for many organizations, there are others where the opportunities to diversify products and services around multiple prices are not as crucial as ensuring that they extract maximum revenue from the facilities provided given the demand. For example, it makes no sense for a restaurant to offer discounts or lower prices during periods of high demand on Friday and Saturday nights. At the same time, we would like to maximize our revenue flows when facilities are fully stretched. This means that there is a strong relationship between average revenue per customer and occupancy rates. While average revenue is the focus of yield management and is visible to customers (and competitors) through pricing strategies, occupancy rates and throughput fall more into the area of process management, to which we turn next.

Process and Project Management (Chapter 4)

Many organizations' activities follow a sequence of events. For example, in a restaurant, a customer arrives, is greeted, is shown to a table, the order is taken, the drinks and food are provided, the bill is presented, and, finally, payment is made and accepted. In busy or peak periods, the duration of time that a table is occupied directly affects the revenue flow. While restaurant managers may feel reluctant to "hurry up" customers, there are areas in the process sequence that can be improved to both reduce meal duration and add value for customers. For example, many restaurants handle presentation of the bill poorly. Customers may be ready to pay, but they often have to wait for attention.

Most people have heard of project management. However, it is usually associated with large construction projects or one-off projects such as convention planning. The sequential nature of processes in most organizations opens the door to using project management to better manage processes, particularly where there are multiple pathways. Mapping the processes and identifying a critical path are easy to do as a first step, with refinements that can include identifying nonvalue-added activities, opportunities to shorten the critical path, and areas where problems can arise—such as a waiter who is trying to take orders, serve meals, bring drinks, bus the tables, and bring the bills all at the same time. Chapter 4 provides some tools and examples of how you can apply project management methods to better manage processes.

Streamlining product offerings in busy periods is another viable strategy for organizations. For a restaurant, reducing choice and standardizing offerings can speed up the menu selection process as well as facilitate food preparation in the kitchen. For professional service firms, such as accountants and doctors, spending time on identifying customer profiles and their needs offers opportunities for improved process flows and greater customer satisfaction. These actions need not lead to lower quality! They simply enable an organization to manage its scope and production more effectively when demand is high.

Capacity and Cost Management (Chapter 5)

The capacity of a business to produce outputs (be they goods or services) constrains managers' freedom of action. Apart from obvious capacity limitations for physical resources such as machinery, building occupancy, and vehicle seating, capacity is also affected by a manager's ability to make appropriate arrangements with suppliers (for example, speed of delivery of raw materials), employees (working hours), and new and existing customers (delivery patterns and service levels). There are also issues relating to defining available capacity and measuring capacity utilization. The capacity constraint represents committed resources, and managers strive to make the best use of these resources because unused capacity represents wasted resources. This is like spending $500 per week for accommodations and only being there half of the time. You might decide that you are happy spending $250 just to retain the accommodation option without using it, or you might look into less expensive or more flexible options, such as spending a bit more but paying only when you use it.

Capacity management plays an important role in organizations that we might not usually regard as having capacity issues—for example, professional services firms such as chartered accountants, lawyers, and consultants. If we consider capacity to be a bundle of services provided by a resource, then it is not difficult to view human resources as possessing the same potential bundle of services. Obtaining the right *mix* and *level* of services is an ongoing task for professional service firms.

We spend money on resources to buy bundles of capacity. It should be apparent that the only way to manage costs, therefore, is to manage resources, and this, in turn, requires management of capacity. We therefore include cost management as part of our capacity management chapter and illustrate how these can be used in conjunction to improve profitability. This requires that we identify the resources consumed and relate them to a cost object (e.g., product or service) and related revenue.

There are some key notions to keep in mind. First, you only manage costs by managing activities. In other words, it is the use of resources by activities (or processes) that gives rise to cost. Consequently, the only way to reduce cost is to reduce the resource consumption by activities. As Chapter 5 points out, identifying cost drivers is a first step in cost management. You must take care if a cost driver is also a revenue driver. Remember that steps to reduce cost will also reduce revenue. Second, activity-based costing (ABC) is tailor-made for understanding how to better manage the activity-resource relationship, and we show how this can be achieved using a combination of high-level concepts and practical examples. Third, you can arrange the activities in ABC models into an ascending hierarchy of levels that captures differences in cost behavior at each level.

The scope or range of services and products can be beneficial in terms of possible cost savings from better use of fixed resources. However, scope can also be a big cost driver, leading to increased complexity in processes and expanding inventory. Gordon Ramsay[5] is an internationally renowned chef who spends part of his time advising struggling restaurants how to turn their businesses around. Invariably, his first step is to examine their menu and reduce the number of items offered. A large menu can mean large quantities of food materials that need to be carried as well as specific processes that need to be performed to produce them. Italian restaurants provide a good example of how to make use of common ingredients (pasta sauces). Similarly, organizations that have a wide range of product offerings often overlook the increased complexity of processes required to support these offerings as well as increased resources in either inventories or specific technology. Note that technology can also include specialized knowledge, such as taxation, governance, research, and development.

Last, but not least, Chapter 6 describes how performance measurement interacts with the other areas to monitor both activities and resource management as well as illuminate areas for improvement.

Performance Measurement (Chapter 6)

Performance measurement frameworks need to address the objectives of stakeholders being served. Thus, when thinking about performance measurement, it is crucial to consider the nature of the performance and the perspective of the particular stakeholder who is interested in the performance. This is crucial when we try to measure performance because we are entering a process of comparing actual events with expectations. What we decide to measure defines what we mean by performance.

However, organizations frequently end up with measurement systems that have just "happened" or that have evolved with too many measures and not enough information. Two major problems are when measures do not reflect the organization or business unit's strategy (i.e., failure to measure effectiveness) and when measures cannot be linked to underlying process drivers (i.e., corrective action is unclear). A more systematic approach that starts with stakeholders and moves through strategy to measures and the drivers of performance is required.

In many circumstances, the main stakeholders are managers either at the operating unit level or at senior levels. Generally, they are concerned with performance that is effective (accomplishes stakeholder goals or needs), efficient (uses minimum input to produce maximum output), and economic (achieves this at "best value"). Chapter 6 discusses performance around three broad areas:

1. Performance measurement frameworks (e.g., the balanced scorecard, linked performance structures incorporating critical success factors, measures, and underlying process drivers)
2. Methods of analysis (e.g., partial productivity measures such as revenue per available unit of capacity, production frontier methods such as data envelopment analysis, simpler analysis methods for aggregating measures)
3. Evaluation processes (analysis is combined with judgment and softer measures)

We describe both financial and nonfinancial measures, explain quantitative as well as qualitative approaches, and show how these can provide effective decision support systems for revenue management.

Summary

We have described revenue management, an exciting area that covers a broad range of topics. This book takes a broad view of revenue management that will enable you to select some of the ideas to trial in your own organization. Keep Figure 1.1 in mind and relate each topic to it. We suggest that it is a good first approach to read the book in sequence, but do feel free to jump about. The final chapter contains a list of key insights from each chapter, which comprises a memory jogger and provides some possible areas to look into when you finish reading this book.

CHAPTER 2

Relating Your Business to Its Environment

Building Strategy From Internal and External Analysis

Introduction

Alice addressed the Cheshire Cat, "Would you tell me, please, which way I ought to go from here?" "That depends a good deal on where you want to get to," said the Cat. "I don't much care where—" said Alice. "Then it doesn't matter which way you go," said the Cat. "—so long as I get somewhere," Alice added as an explanation. "Oh, you're sure to do that," said the Cat.

—Lewis Carroll, *Alice in Wonderland*

Some businesspeople are opportunistic—they take advantage of opportunities as they arise. Although Alice appears happy to get somewhere, and it apparently does not matter where, most people have some idea of what they seek, and they are most likely to achieve this by deciding on a way of getting there—a set of strategies or a strategic plan.

Strategy relates to the fit between an organization and its environment. The better the fit, the better the strategy. In formulating a strategy, look outward to the environment and inward to the organization. To manage revenue successfully, an organization should understand its environment and adapt its strategy in terms of pricing and internal organization. For example, in an imperfect market, a business might decide that because it has a cost advantage, it will price below the market price and maximize revenue (and profit) through high volumes. Another business may select a particular feature of its product or service, which it will focus on and charge a higher price than the market. From an internal perspective, a business needs to ensure that it aligns processes and capabilities with its strategies, especially pricing. Pricing above market implies that the product or service has quality features that others do not possess; they must deliver on this notion or the strategy will fail. Some organizations are especially good at particular things, such as order taking, delivery, reliability of service, or product. These competencies provide an organization with an advantage that it can exploit in order to achieve greater revenues and profits. Knowing an organization's strengths and weaknesses is the first step in identifying its competencies as a basis for its strategies, of which revenue management is a central part. This chapter seeks to describe, define, and illustrate key components of a strategic framework for revenue and cost management.

SWOT Analysis and Some Terms Used in Strategy

We all have strengths and weaknesses—they enable us to perform well when we employ our strengths and not so well when we rely on weaknesses. So it is with a business; once we know the strengths and weaknesses, we are in a position to build on strengths and neutralize or strengthen weaknesses. One way to identify an organization's strengths and weaknesses is to focus on its functional areas—top management, operations, marketing, human resources, and finance-accounting—and pinpoint those aspects that it handles well, not so well, or poorly. You also need to look outside the organization, to the environment, to identify opportunities and threats. We refer to this as a SWOT analysis—an analysis of strengths, weaknesses, opportunities, and threats. Strengths and weaknesses refer to the internal characteristics of an organization while opportunities and threats refer to the external features of its environment.

A SWOT analysis helps to answer the following types of questions:

- Does the organization have strengths on which to build an attractive strategy?
- Which weaknesses should a strategy correct?
- Do the organization's weaknesses disqualify it from pursuing certain opportunities?
- Which opportunities does the organization have the resources to pursue with a chance of success?
- About which threats should the organization worry most?

A SWOT analysis produces insights into the fit between the organization and its environment and enables you to sketch the strategy by which to move forward. In the case study at the end of the chapter, we illustrate a SWOT analysis and the development of strategies by referring to a short case, Toulette's Stores.

Many organizations have invested considerable effort in formalizing strategy by means of mission statements, goals, and objectives. The main purpose is to ensure that everyone within the organization understands what it is trying to achieve and that their efforts are aligned with strategy at all levels. When reading about strategy, you will find that different authors define terms to suit their various messages and frequently use the terms "mission," "goals," "objectives," "policy," and "strategy" interchangeably. This may be confusing. Following the main thrust of the following definition, we adopt a standard set of definitions in this book:

> Strategy is the forging of company mission, setting objectives for the organization in light of external and internal forces, formulating specific policies and strategies to achieve objectives, and assuring their proper implementation so that the basic purposes and objectives of the organization will be achieved.[1]

While many organizations have a vision and a mission statement, the difference between them is often unclear. The mission statement is a broad declaration of the basic, unique purpose and scope of operations that distinguishes the organization from others of its type.[2] In contrast to the "doing" flavor of the mission statement, the vision refers to what the organization might look like in a desirable future state. "Policies" is another term that is often unclear. We interpret policies as guides to action or channels to thinking. At high levels, policies are indistinguishable from strategies; lower-level policies have less scope and importance and fade into procedures and rules.[3]

Policies are especially important in revenue management, as they not only communicate the revenue management strategy but also outline the rules that need to be complied with. For example, Chapter 3 describes the way in which airlines segment their markets using rules such as cheaper advance-purchase tickets that must be booked and paid for 3 weeks before the departure date. If the booking agent does not abide by the policy (or rule, in this case), the entire revenue management strategy is undermined. This is a serious problem in the hotel industry, where policies with respect to lower price options are regularly broken.

The meanings of the terms in Figure 2.1 appear in Table 2.1.[4] Figure 2.1 depicts a strategic process whereby the organization states its vision, sets its mission, goals, and objectives, taking into consideration the expectations and needs of target groups and stakeholders and its environmental context. Part of the strategic process encompasses the setting of plans and policies for the attainment of goals and objectives.

This seems to imply that strategy is fairly mechanistic and follows a logical sequence of steps. In practice, we develop strategy through multiple iterations, with many changes and revisions to the initial assumptions. Some organizations face reasonably stable environments and follow a "classical" approach, where the plans emerging from the process in Figure 2.1 are implemented and followed over a period of time. Others face environments that are constantly changing, which require them to follow what is called an "emergent" approach. Although they follow the process in Figure 2.1, everything is subject to change. They modify plans and adapt to changes in the game plan; strategy is thus made more through action than initial planning.

You can enhance the external and internal orientation of SWOT by adopting more specialized approaches, namely, industry analysis and core

Table 2.1. List of Terms for Figure 2.1

Vision:	An overriding idea of what the organization should be
Mission:	The organization's purpose or fundamental reason for existence
Values:	The principles or beliefs that represent what an organization stands for and how it will operate
Goal:	A future target or end result that an organization wishes to achieve, which is of a general nature and long-lived
Objective:	A specific target with a short to medium time horizon, which is envisaged as contributing toward the attainment of a goal or goals
Strategy:	The process of identifying the mission and specifying goals that provide the directions indicated by the mission, together with the setting of objectives and plans for their attainment
Plan:	A course of action to attain one or more objectives, which usually includes specific performance norms
Policy:	Procedures or rules that provide guides to action or channels to thinking in line with plans and objectives

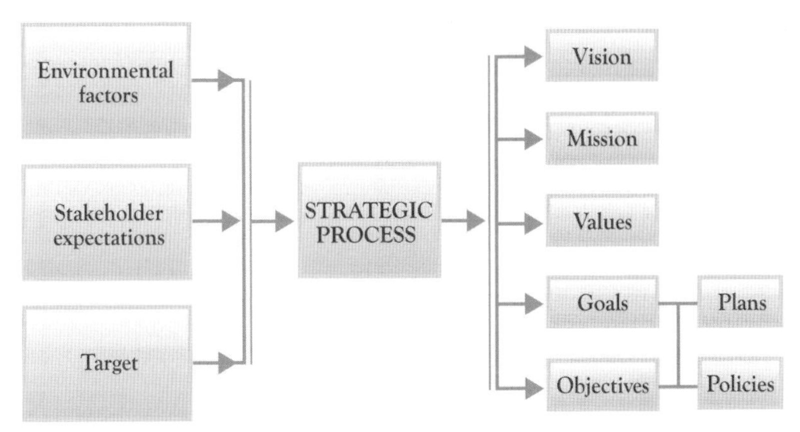

Figure 2.1. The strategic process of stating vision and setting the mission, goals, objectives, plans, and policies

competence. But how do you make this happen? Involvement and participation promotes buy-in and improves implementation. These aspects are covered later in this chapter.

Industry Analysis: The Five Competitive Forces

As described in the introduction to this chapter, a thorough SWOT analysis provides a sound foundation for the development of strategies. While the management in our case study, Toulette's Stores, commenced with an internal analysis—strengths and weaknesses—they could equally have chosen to start with an external analysis, which focuses on opportunities and threats. Irrespective of where they start, managers can extend or confirm their external analysis by using Porter's approach to industry analysis.[5] Porter identifies five major competitive forces that determine the parameters for the potential profitability of an industry. The five forces are threat of new entrants (or barriers to entry), bargaining power of suppliers, bargaining power of buyers (customers), threat of substitutes and rivalry (competition) within the industry (see Figure 2.2). It is easy to see how this impacts revenue management. For example, the threat of new entrants and rivalry directly impact the pricing levels within the industry. The higher the rivalry, the more downward pressure there is on prices. If barriers to entry are high, then the incumbent businesses can pursue more independent pricing strategies without worrying about newcomers undermining their business.

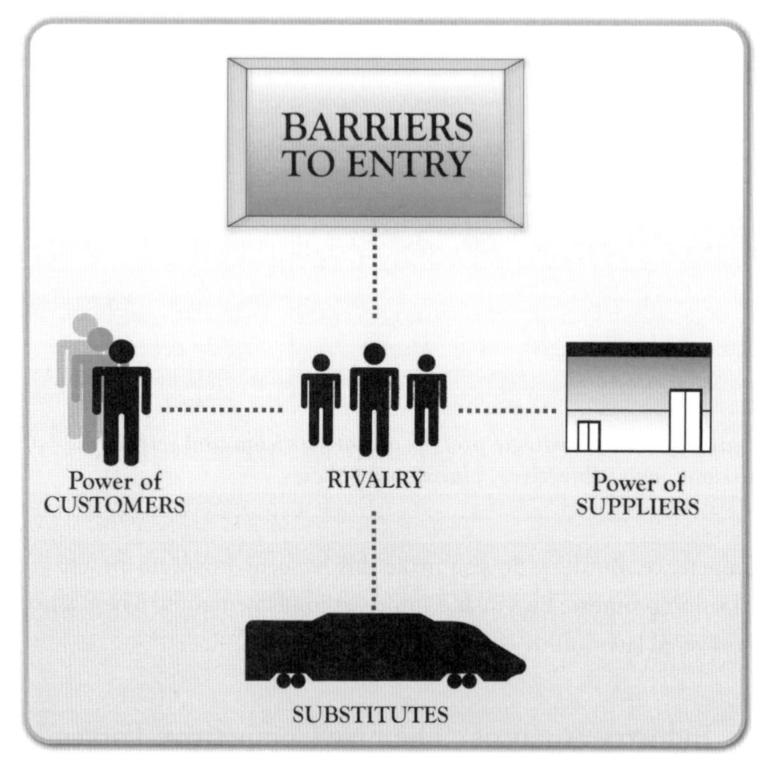

Figure 2.2. Five forces for assessing industry profitability

In an extreme case, an organization would find itself in a desperate situation if the industry in which it operates manifests intense rivalry, strong bargaining power on the part of both suppliers and buyers, readily available substitutes for its products and services, and low barriers to entry, which indicates a high threat of new entrants. The converse would indicate an attractive industry. In practice, there is likely to be a mix of conditions, and with careful analysis, this situation provides pointers for the appropriate strategic positioning in order to gain competitive advantage. For example, in Toulette's Stores' niche: the threat of new entrants is high (i.e., the barriers to entry are low), although reputation in the market and strong buying skills may ameliorate this threat to some extent; both the power of suppliers and rivalry are relatively weak; and substitutes are not plentiful.

Porter suggests three generic strategies from which an organization can select in a bid to achieve competitive advantage. These are cost leadership, differentiation, and scope (see Figure 2.3). A cost leader broadly focuses on achieving the lowest cost in its market segment; it gains and maintains competitive advantage through lower costs than those of its rivals. It can therefore set its prices below those of its competitors in order to achieve higher volumes and still obtain a superior profit since it has lower costs. If an organization chooses to pursue a differentiation strategy, it focuses on making its products or services different from those of its rivals. It may do this through special features, product or service quality, distribution channels, or customer support. This difference is, in itself, not sufficient for gaining competitive advantage—the differentiation must be such that the organization's consumers are happy to pay a premium for the product or service. The organization therefore sets its prices above those of its competitors, and although the additional features or quality that differentiate it may result in increased costs, its prices should be set sufficiently high to offset these and achieve superior profits. The characteristics of cost leader and differentiator carry through to the focus variations—the only difference lies in the competitive scope—whether it chooses a narrow or a broad target (see Figure 2.3). For example, Figure 2.3 illustrates the application of these strategies to the oil industry, where an organization follows a broad-scope cost leadership strategy by controlling all aspects from drilling to the gas pump and creating competitive advantage through economies of scale. The broad-scope differentiator controls all aspects from drilling through refinery and creates competitive advantage through developing new products or new refinery processes. Organizations following a narrow scope might focus only on drilling, with a cost-focused provider creating competitive advantage through the use of low-cost labor and a differentiator creating its advantage through the use of innovative drilling technology.

In our case study, Toulette's Stores has essentially positioned itself with a low-cost focus in its retail segment. It remains to be seen whether the company will be able to maintain its cost leadership in light of the new elements of its strategy. We should recognize that cost leadership does not necessarily imply poor quality—a cost leader still needs to meet the quality expectations of customers for the prices charged. Likewise, a differentiator does not ignore cost; however, the organization adds cost only to the extent that the premium justifies it.

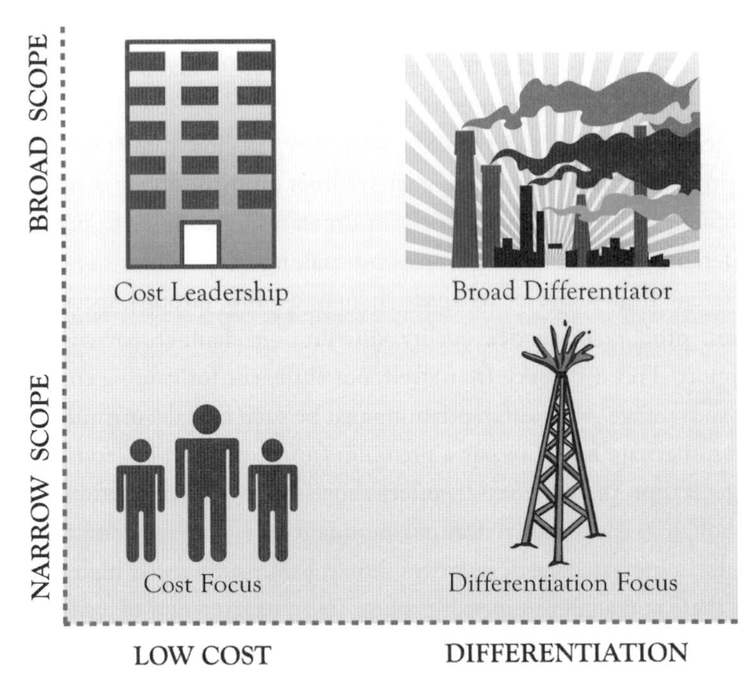

Figure 2.3. Generic strategies for competitive advantage

Porter's approach has clear implications for revenue management, as the industry analysis and competitive positioning impact directly on pricing and the way the business organizes its internal processes.

Porter is emphatic that an organization must choose one of these three strategies. Success requires a single-minded pursuit of the chosen positioning strategy. If the organization attempts to follow a low cost and a differentiation strategy at the same time, it will fail to gain competitive advantage. Porter refers to this as being "stuck in the middle." Other authors have subsequently identified organizations that have apparently been successful both in achieving low cost and in differentiating their product or service.

Cooper and Slagmulder[6] suggest that both low cost and differentiation strategies will inevitably be confrontational in a competitive market. They work through target costing and value engineering to identify the survival triplet, which comprises cost (price), functionality, and quality or reliability. Organizations must compete on all three dimensions within their survival zones. The range of the variables within the survival zone narrows as the intensity of confrontation increases. These confrontational strategies demand that organizations focus on low cost and differentiation at the same time, which is contrary to Porter's advice.

One such example is Toyota (we restrict our attention to the period before Toyota's recent safety defects). Toyota was able to produce a low-cost vehicle and to differentiate it in terms of quality. Porter's advice nevertheless has merit. Being stuck in the middle is a real possibility if the organization is not clear on its positioning and the necessary activities to achieve and maintain it. The key message is to ensure your strategy is clear on what you want to do, why you want to do it, and how you are going to do it.

Management can gain further significant insights for gaining competitive advantage by analyzing the organization's value chain (or, in a multibusiness organization, the value chains of individual strategic business units).[7] The strength of a value-chain analysis is that it focuses specifically on the very items that compose the process side of revenue management (refer back to Figure 1.1). Managers analyze each process and activity in terms of what it contributes to the end value to the customer. We will see that this is particularly important in Chapter 4 when we discuss identifying nonvalue-adding activities.

In constructing the value chain for a strategic business unit, we identify its activities and distinguish between primary and support activities (see Figure 2.4). Primary activities comprise developing the product or service to meet customer needs (research and development), organizing and managing resources to ensure the product or service can be delivered (resource coordination), marketing, producing and delivering the product or service, and customer (relationship) management. Support activities include human resource management, procurement, information technology, strategy, and senior management. Linkages among activities provide opportunities for obtaining competitive advantage.

As each organization has a value chain, an industry comprises a number of value chains, frequently called a value system, as depicted in the lower part of Figure 2.4. Although one organization may undertake all the value-adding activities shown in Figure 2.4, this need not be the case; separate strategic business units (SBUs) may be responsible for different upstream and downstream activities. Organizations configure primary activities according to the main thrust of their business. For example, primary activities such as inbound and outbound logistics in primary

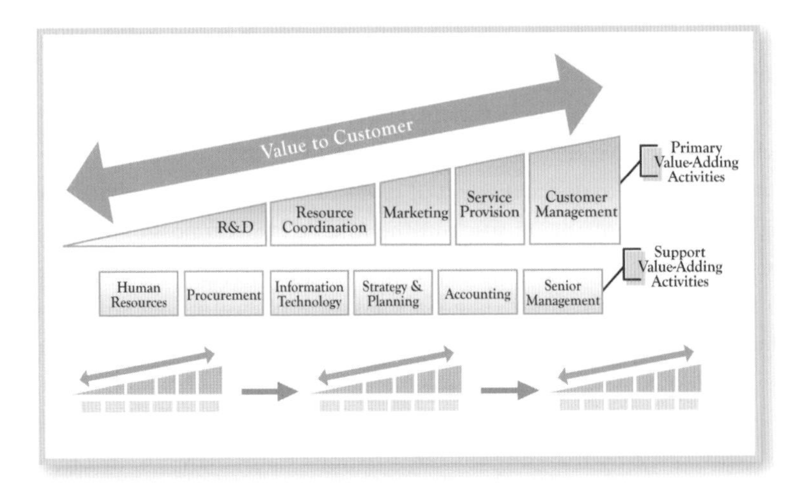

Figure 2.4. Upstream and downstream value activities

producers in the food industry (farmers and processing plants) are similar to those in manufacturing. Resource coordination in a service organization such as a restaurant tends to comprise more management activities, such as scheduling and organizing resources, than we would otherwise expect.

Figure 2.5 depicts the value system for the restaurant industry. The primary level constitutes agribusiness, including growing and harvesting crops, animal husbandry, and killing and processing, while wholesalers pack products and distribute them to restaurants for eventual service to customers. Different firms focus on particular parts of this value system. For example, Firm D is confined to the restaurant part of the system while Firm A extends across the entire industry. In some countries, McDonald's might be an example of Firm A, whereas Firm D might be your local restaurant.

The value system appears very similar to a supply chain. Feller, Shunk, and Callarman[8] draw a useful distinction between supply chains and value chains. Supply chains focus upstream on integrating supplier and producer processes, with the objective of improving efficiencies and reducing waste. In Figure 2.5, they can be viewed as starting from the top (farming) and working downward to improve interactions among the various segments (e.g., farming and harvesting). In contrast, value chains focus downstream on creating value for the customer. In Figure 2.5, we start with the end customer and work upward to evaluate each element of each segment in terms

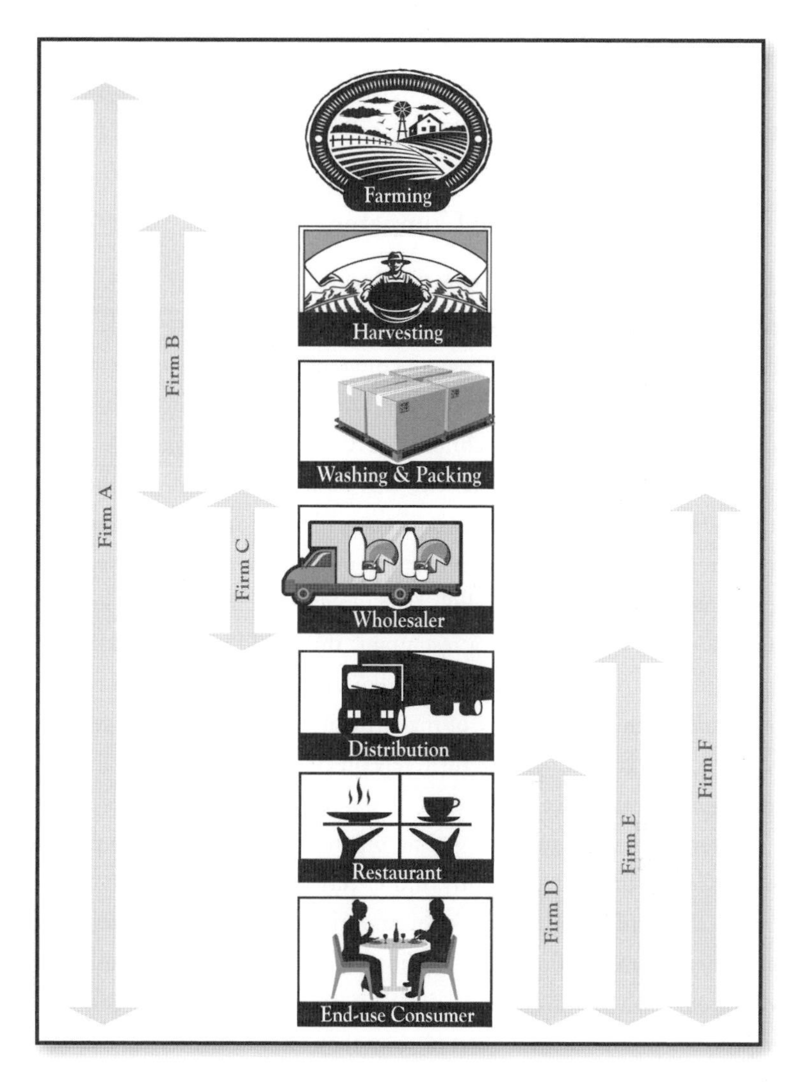

Figure 2.5. The value system for the restaurant industry

of its contribution to the end value. Feller et al. (2006) sum this up nicely: "Creating a profitable value chain therefore requires alignment between what the customer wants, i.e., the demand chain, and what is produced via the supply chain. And while supply chains focus primarily on reducing costs and attaining operational excellence, value chains focus more on innovation in product development and marketing."

The strategic business unit is at the center of Porter's approach, which provides a useful framework for categorizing organizational strategies observed in practice. While this framework evolves from an external perspective, Prahalad and Hamel[9] develop the concept of core competence from an internal orientation.

Core Competencies

Core competence is about communication, involvement, and a deep commitment to working across organizational boundaries. While procedures, systems, and people generate core competencies, they are mainly people-based, emanating from organizational learning that facilitates the coordination of skills and technologies. Underlying competitive advantage is a level of core competencies that competitors find it difficult to achieve. It is important for organizations to identify and understand these competencies so that they can retain and nurture them. We envisage core competencies as the essential skills for a service organization that keep the customers coming back. For a restaurant, this could be the cooking, the waiter service, or even the ambiance. For an airline, the core competencies could be the high quality of the airplanes and in-flight service, or its safety record, which might, in turn, rely on core competencies in its flight crews and maintenance activities.

Revenue management relies on an organization's capability to provide the service or product efficiently and effectively. The best pricing structure in the world will not work for an airline that is not able to get its passengers from location A to location B. At the same time, customers will often select a business that possesses an ability to get the job done or product produced in a "better" way than other businesses. Many of us prefer to fly with some airlines because of superior in-flight service (friendly cabin crew are a special reason) or we just feel more confident in the capability of the airline.

According to Prahalad and Hamel,[10]

> The diversified corporation is a large tree. The trunk and major limbs are core products, the smaller branches are business units; the leaves, flowers, and fruit are end products. The root system that provides nourishment, sustenance and stability is the core competence. You can miss the strength of competitors by looking

only at their end products, in the same way you miss the strength of a tree if you look only at its leaves.

Figure 2.6 depicts the end products or services as leaves on a tree, which result from a combination of core products and the organization's internal processes. In the example of an airline, this combination of core products and internal processes could be its maintenance or training of its flight crew. Underpinning these processes are the roots of the tree, that is, the competencies that distinguish the business from others.

How do organizations develop and retain these competencies? For many, training of employees is an essential tool, but this is not sufficient. There are more subtle requirements, such as coordination and communication processes. In fact, effective coordination processes are probably a key requirement for any organization in developing, nurturing, and retaining core competencies. Prahalad and Hamel,[11] who see the company in terms of a portfolio of competencies, underscore the importance of coordination. They suggest that a company's core competencies are its critical resources, and that it is top management's responsibility to ensure that some particular business does not exclusively hold those competence carriers. It follows that core competencies are corporate resources, that

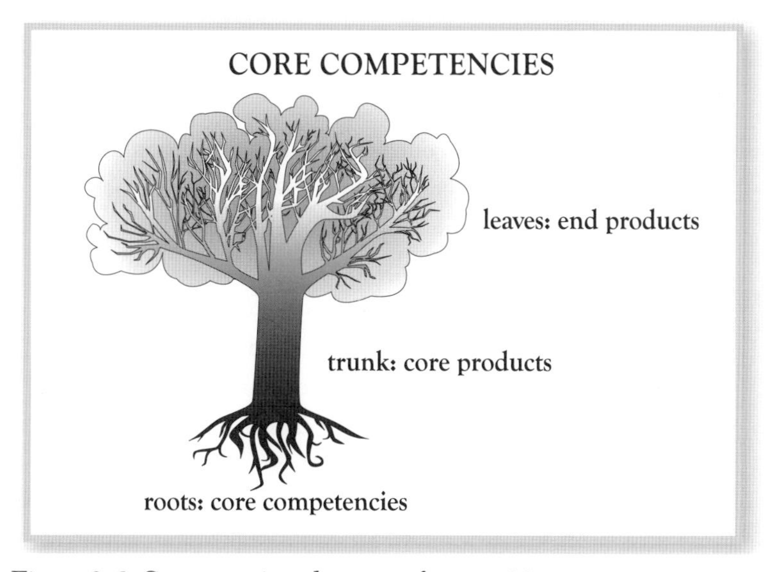

Figure 2.6. Competencies: the roots of competitiveness

corporate management may reallocate them, and that SBUs should bid for core competencies in the same way they bid for capital.

Blue ocean strategy combines the external views of Porter and the internally focused core competencies of Prahalad and Hamel. The implication for revenue management is that it provides tools for analyzing an organization's environment as well as exploring actions to be taken to optimize value, which can be interpreted as increasing revenue without deteriorating costs and investment.

Blue Ocean Strategy

I must go down to the seas again, to the lonely sea and the sky,
And all I ask is a tall ship and a star to steer her by.

—John Masefield, "Sea Fever"

The notion of the deep blue ocean may be appealing—the openness of the sea and the sky bring images of freedom, isolation, and adventure. For Kim and Mauborgne,[12] the blue ocean is the metaphor for uncontested market space. In contrast, when organizations are continuously in intense cutthroat competition, the ocean is red with the blood of the battle. The authors make the following comments about blue ocean strategy (BOS) on their website:

- BOS is the simultaneous pursuit of differentiation and low cost.
- The aim of BOS is not to out-perform the competition in the existing industry, but to create new market space or a blue ocean, thereby making the competition irrelevant.
- While innovation has been seen as a random/experimental process where entrepreneurs and spin-offs are the primary drivers—as argued by Schumpeter and his followers—BOS offers systematic and reproducible methodologies and processes in pursuit of blue oceans by both new and existing firms.[13]

Kim and Mauborgne investigate 108 launches of new companies and find that 86% of them represent an extension of existing market space. This accounts for 62% of total revenue and 39% of total profit of the sample group. On the other hand, blue oceans account for 38% of total revenue and 61% of total profit for the sample group. The evidence that a blue ocean strategy brings superior results is compelling. Kim and Mauborgne develop concepts and practical guidelines for blue ocean strategy through a study of 150 strategic moves over a period of more than 100 years. They refer to *strategic move* as a set of actions and decisions that management makes when it makes a business offering leading to the creation of a major market. Their use of the strategic move as the unit of analysis contrasts with other approaches that focus on either the company or the industry.

One of the key tools used in blue ocean strategy is the strategy canvas. Figure 2.7 depicts a strategy canvas for Southwest Airlines, showing eight dimensions in the industry that an organization can compete on. These are shown on the horizontal axis and include price, meals, lounges, and so on. The stacked bars represent the relative focus of three alternatives on each of these dimensions. The three alternatives are the average airline, Southwest Airlines, and a substitute, which is travel by car.

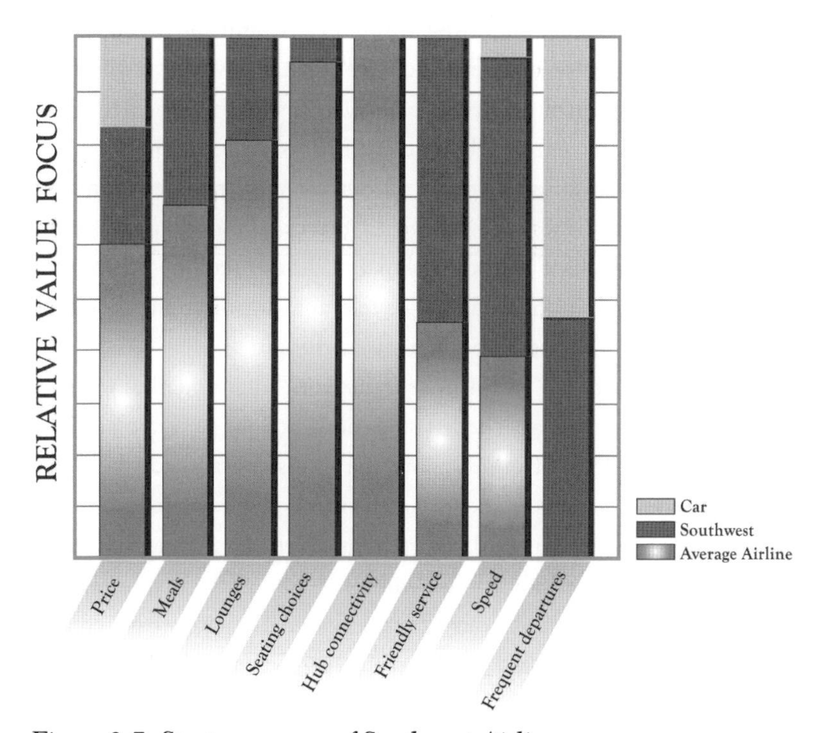

Figure 2.7. Strategy canvas of Southwest Airlines

Southwest and the car substitute have much lower prices (i.e., cost to the customer) than the average airline, shown by the relative size of the first bar components. They also have much less emphasis on lounges, meals, and seating choices (none in the case of car transport).[14] Kim and Mauborgne point out that this strategy canvas reveals three characteristics of a good strategy: focus, divergence, and a compelling tag line. In comparison with the average airlines representing the industry, Southwest Airlines clearly emphasizes friendly service, speed, and frequent point-to-point departures. This focus means that it does not devote resources to meals, lounges, and similar items, allowing it to price against car transportation. Across the various features of air travel, it is vastly different compared with the average airlines, leading to the second characteristic.

A blue ocean strategy demands uniqueness—a move away from attempting to keep up with competing companies. This reflects the second characteristic—divergence. Southwest Airlines clearly illustrates divergence by placing much less emphasis on the factors common to other industry players such as business-class lounges and meals. Finally, the authors suggest that Southwest Airlines can command a compelling tag line: "The speed of a plane at the price of a car—whenever you need it." It would be difficult to devise a similarly distinctive tag line for the other airlines. Kim and Mauborgne see this as value innovation—the simultaneous quest to reduce cost and increase value requires alignment of all the firm's activities with this goal. Porter's admonition against the simultaneous pursuit of cost leadership and differentiation—often leading to being "stuck in the middle"—is relevant; organizations should be clear about their strategies in order to avoid this pitfall.

Figure 2.8 depicts a "four actions framework" that underlies what we see in the strategic canvas. The left side shows actions to create new factors or raise the level of others above the industry standard; the right-hand side shows actions that eliminate existing factors or reduce others to below the industry standard. We see that Southwest Airlines has eliminated factors that the industry has embraced and, at the same time, has introduced factors that the industry has not offered. Factors to be reduced below the industry standard are matched with factors to be raised above the industry standard. This is the basis for carefully managing opposite actions, rather than simply performing a balancing act. This fits with the

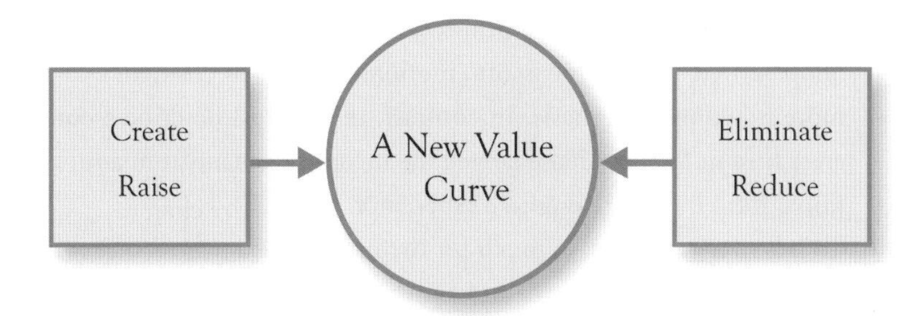

Figure 2.8. The four actions framework

revenue management notions laid out in Figure 1.1, which combine the external and internal features that an organization needs to consider.

We can see the four actions framework reflected in Southwest Airlines' strategy canvas. Southwest Airlines has eliminated hub connectivity, seating-class choices, and lounges, and has created frequent point-to-point departures. It has reduced its in-flight amenities (no meals, although they provide free peanuts and other snacks) and raised friendly service and speed well above the industry standards. Southwest Airlines has been able to raise and create factors, which achieve differentiation, and to reduce and eliminate other factors, which achieves cost reduction. This has not resulted in being "stuck in the middle."

It is essential to reconstruct market boundaries in the pursuit of blue ocean strategy. The authors describe six paths, which involve examining slices of industries, groupings, product categories, and the like to gain insights. Briefly, these are as follows:

1. Alternative industries. For example, cinemas versus restaurants or the airline versus the car.
2. Strategic groups. For example, the Walkman revolutionized the way people listened to music. A similar thing has happened with the iPod and iTunes.
3. The chain of buyers. For example, instead of selling insulin to medical practitioners, a major supplier provided an easy-to-use insulin dispenser that could be sold directly to the public.
4. Complementary product and service offerings. For example, imagine a cinema that also offers babysitting services.

5. Functional or emotional appeal to buyers. For example, The Body Shop moved from a focus on emotional appeal of cosmetics to a more functional emphasis. In contrast, the authors describe a concrete firm in Mexico that changed the image of cement from a functional form to a more emotive experience.
6. Trends over time, not so much for themselves but for how they will change value to customers and impact on the company's business model.

We have presented some of the key points on which Kim and Mauborgne build blue ocean strategy; their book contains considerable further material. Cirque du Soleil's blue ocean strategy is a fitting conclusion to this section of our chapter on strategy. Cirque du Soleil created a new industry, achieving both differentiation and low cost; it reinvented the circus market by attracting a clientele that would probably not have gone to a traditional circus. Cirque du Soleil excludes animals, multiple show areas, and star performers—all high-cost elements. At the same time, it avoids criticism usually leveled at circuses with performing animals. The tent, the clowns, and the acrobatic acts preserve the atmosphere of the circus, while the tent itself has a glamorous external finish and comfortable seating. Drawing from the theater, the circus features stories, music, and dance. This justifies prices aligned with the theater rather than the circus. As mentioned earlier, the coexistence of differentiation and cost reduction in blue ocean strategy defies Porter's admonitions of being "stuck in the middle." It provides a compatible model for the revenue management theme of this book.

The difficulty with the models and frameworks presented in this chapter is that they do not just happen. Employees do not immediately buy into strategy and usually do not understand it; at worst, they ignore it. Chapter 3 describes the more formal side of yield management, and you will see that it relies on what we call "sorting mechanisms" to segment markets with different product definitions. One of the major problems that organizations (particularly hotels) face is employees ignoring these sorting mechanisms. Getting the whole organization aligned is difficult, and there are various approaches to achieving this. We conclude this chapter by describing one process for getting strategy—in particular, revenue management—into your organization, although it can be used for implementing any new concept or idea.

The Search Conference

In the movie *Shirley Valentine*, Shirley's headmistress asks, "What was man's most important invention?"[15] Shirley knows the answer, is deliberately ignored, and when finally allowed to provide the "correct" answer, she is labeled a cheat. Although most people are not called cheats in their organizations, many feel that managers ignore their ideas about strategy.

We use the word "strategy" all the time in business, but when it comes to the crunch, how do we make it happen? How can an organization get all its employees on board and speaking the same language? Why do so many efforts at strategy not work very well? Why do our vision statements, mission statements, and goals sound suspiciously the same as everyone else's? Why do most strategic plans sound like empty generalizations?

There are major reasons why organizations struggle to get successful strategic frameworks in place. First, too many strategic efforts fail to place the target organization in its context. In other words, those responsible for strategy frequently neglect to perform a systematic and wide-ranging scan of the environment. Most organizations tend to focus inwardly, and even when they look externally, they concentrate on the immediate surroundings and overlook the broader changes occurring in the world. Second, organizations often ignore their "Shirley Valentines," that is, they pay insufficient attention to insights offered by their own people. What is worse is that they fail to recognize that a "shared" view of the world is a prerequisite to planning long-term directions. People need a common language to express their dreams!

Third, organizations often underestimate the importance of the process and go for the quick-fix solution. Anyone can sit down and dream up some goals and label them as strategy, but they will remain dreams unless processes are implemented to convert them into actions. The processes we have in mind include the development of the strategic direction, action groups, templates, planned forums, staff training, and education.

To develop a successful strategy, we need a process that provides the following features:

- An emerging common objective based on a shared view of the world
- Trust and cooperation

- A common language
- Acceptance of the importance of shared dreams
- An appreciation of the milestones, pitfalls, and skills required for the journey

The search conference method[16] directly addresses the aforementioned features in both practical and theoretical terms. It is a participative event that enables a large group to collectively create a plan that its members will implement. It is an approach to *planned change* that engages the collective learning and creativity of large groups, inspiring people to find common ground among new strategies, future directions, and joint actions. There are many supporting elements from systems theory and group dynamics, but most of this boils down to a few solid principles.

First, an open system[17] must maintain an adaptive relationship with its environment. As a first step in any search conference, participants carry out a far-ranging scan of their environment. Organizations tend to forget that staff read newspapers, scientific and business magazines, watch television news and documentaries, as well as listen to radio broadcasts. They are usually well informed and have clear and accurate perceptions of changes in their environment. Listening to these perceptions and constructing a database of environmental change is not only low cost but also relevant to the organization, since they will already have filtered and interpreted world events in light of their personal circumstances, which includes membership in the organization.

Second, every person attending a search conference is considered an expert. The purpose, or conference task, sets the criteria for participant selection. Loosely, those who are in a position to take responsibility for the fate and survival of an organization are in; those who are not are out!

Third, every participant's contribution is valued and is shared openly. There are no notetakers or hidden agendas in search conferences. All information is recorded on clipboards and displayed on surrounding walls. In this way, participants are surrounded by their own creations.

This third point needs further explanation. To build democracy and trust, participants need assurance that their surroundings are open and equally accessible to all of them. There is no hidden agenda, manipulation, or concealment of information. Instead, participants realize that they live in a similar world and experience similar hopes and fears. In this way, a shared view of the world is created.

Every search conference is unique, requiring special planning and design. There are no standardized guidebooks or worksheets to take off the shelf and apply to every situation—those who want to learn how to manage and design search conferences need to understand the underlying theory.[18] Nonetheless, it is possible to summarize the general flow of a search conference, which is depicted in Figure 2.9 in the form of a funnel.

Participants begin with activities designed to help them learn about what is happening in their environment, which is called "environmental scanning." For example, in a search conference we facilitated, this was fun and informative. Responses were fast and furious, and we compiled over 20 pages of clipboard charts within 20 minutes. We then pasted these on the wall and asked participants to wander about and think of

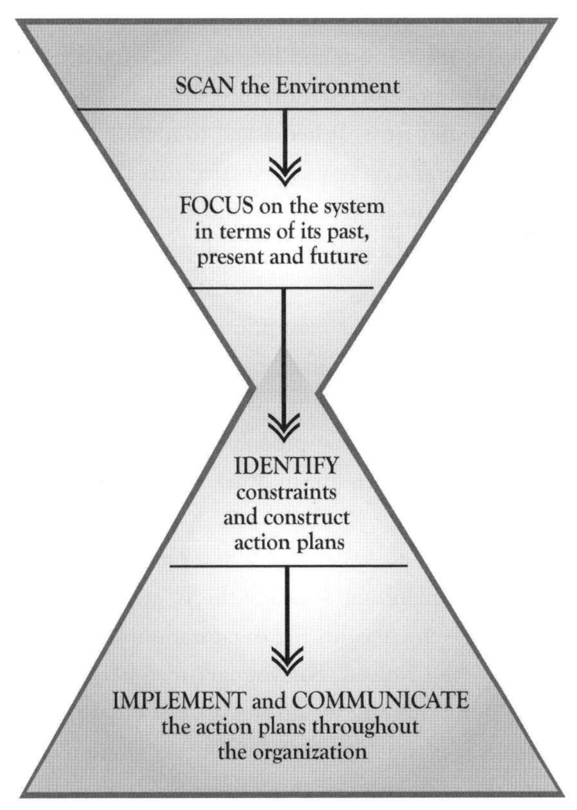

Figure 2.9. Funnel diagram of the search conference

ways of categorizing these items into broader categories. These categories from the environmental scan included globalization, technology (e-commerce), lifestyle, and company responsibility. These were typical issues, but, more importantly, they were gleaned from the participants themselves! The results of the environmental scan provided an excellent status report of their environment and how it interacted with their organization. We doubt that a report prepared by external consultants would have added much to this, and it certainly would not have attained the same level of agreement and comprehension.

As part of the environmental scanning, the workshop can be divided into smaller groups in order to consider desirable and probable states. Each group is provided with a flip chart on which to write their output for presentation to the combined groups. This stage introduces "value" judgments into the process in the form of desirable changes in our world. The probable states are introduced to provide a counterpoint to the desirable changes. The feeling of the workshop becomes more emotive in terms of despair, frustration, and helplessness. Notwithstanding, two very important outcomes emerge from this part of the process. First, participants begin to build trust. When asked to identify what is going on in the world, most people do not feel worried that their observations are going to be argued against or rejected. Commenting on something taking place on the other side of the world feels distant enough that everyone feels comfortable contributing to the discussion. Participants also begin to realize that they have similar perceptions of what is happening in the world. Second, they begin to realize that they have similar dreams and values about how they would like the world to be, while understanding that without positive action, the probable outcome will be something that none of them would wish for. In other words, they begin to acquire a shared view of the world.

Next, they explore their system's past and present as a prelude to the future and long-range planning. Much of this is "storytelling" by employees about their involvement with the organization and various histories with which they were involved. For younger members, this can explain why things are "done the way we do them." For older members, it can show that perhaps it is time to move on! The exploration of the current system leads to the same ways of thinking as the blue ocean method—create, drop, raise, and lower actions. This is where companies create or raise value while lowering costs. For example, in the workshop we facilitated, participants decided to create a new interface with clients using web technology, increased the creative design activities of the organization, and reduced the size of the traditional production department. The future component involves the development of strategic goals for creating a desirable future for the organization's system, along with action plans that need to consider obstacles and what resources need to be created. After the conference, the group works to ensure that others become involved in the implementation and diffusion of the strategic plan.

Time wise, roughly a third of the conference focuses on learning about changes and trends in the environment. Another third is spent on looking at the system—its past history, its present strengths and weaknesses, and its most desirable future. The last third of the conference shifts into high gear, as future visions are reality-tested against existing constraints and action-planning groups figure out how to implement their strategic goals.

By this time, the members of the organization have created their own language, and although their goals might look like textbook goals, they still have distinctive meaning to the conference participants. Many organizations, including Microsoft, have used the search conference when searching for an appropriate response to the arrival of the Internet.

Summary

Chapter 2 has briefly described some of the major aspects of strategy that are relevant to revenue management. SWOT, five-forces industry analysis, core competencies, blue ocean strategy, and the search conference are all powerful aids for understanding and developing strategy. Each of these, in its own way, can be located within Figure 1.1. Nonetheless, the challenge lies in the application of these tools. However, success in this regard provides insights that are potentially valuable in enhancing understanding and initiating improvements.

The content of this chapter is not comprehensive. Examples of other models that come to mind are the Miles and Snow typology[19] of firms into prospectors, defenders, analyzers, and reactors; PESTEL or PESTLE (political, environmental, social, technological, ecological, and legal) analysis; and scenario planning. The references and the Internet are good sources from which to obtain further information about strategy and related issues.

Next, we turn to more specific strategic decisions around pricing and to extracting the maximum revenue possible without incurring excessive cost or investment outlays.

Key Insights

- Understand your organization's environment and context. Use the available tools to analyze an organization's environment.
  - Start with SWOT—it is easy to do and always provides insights.
  - Use Porter's industry analysis to analyze the external environment in which your organization operates.
  - Identify your existing core competences. Later, you can identify if you need to develop new ones.
- Use Porter's competitive positioning or the blue ocean tools to identify what you should do. (We favor blue ocean, but Porter's model is still in operation in many organizations.)
- Use the strategic elements depicted in Figure 2.1 to formulate your strategy or to evaluate your current strategy.
- Embed revenue management in the strategy from the objectives and planning to the detailed policies.
- Communicate and obtain buy-in from employees. This is *the* critical success factor. Processes like the search conference can overcome resistance and inertia while ensuring that communication and buy-in are achieved.

Case Study: Toulette's Stores[20]

Xou-Xou Toulette was a top buyer in a leading department store in Melbourne, which is the largest city in the state of Victoria in Australia. She regularly traveled overseas, attending trade fairs and contracting with overseas suppliers. She has a reputation for being a tough negotiator but a fair and ethical businessperson. Believing that there was a niche in the marketplace for a discount operation specializing in toiletries, she resigned from her position in 1990 and opened a store in one of Melbourne's busy shopping malls.

One of Xou-Xou's basic revenue management principles is to keep prices lower than other retailers and to earn a reputation for value for money in the field of toiletries. To achieve these objectives, she traveled overseas and negotiated keen prices, but only on lines that supported themselves and achieved targeted returns. She chose products on the basis of high-volume potential and did not carry any line simply because it was part of the range. House brands were not a feature of her merchandising policy. Xou-Xou kept a close watch on competitors' prices to ensure that Toulette's Stores remained the cheapest. She did not offer credit to customers, and this helped to maintain low prices.

After operating for one year, during which the business flourished, Xou-Xou opened three new stores in the Melbourne suburbs. She relied on her cousins and profit retentions to finance this expansion—her cousins invested capital in the business without being active in its management. To duplicate the success of the original store, Xou-Xou selected buyers with excellent track records whom she knew and in whom she could place her full trust to manage the new stores.

On account of Xou-Xou's excellent reputation with her suppliers, the business received their support throughout the rapid expansion of the following years. By 1995, the company had expanded to a chain of 10 stores, extending throughout the state, and had stuck to what she saw as a winning formula—the limited product range at low prices, in unpretentious trading premises with small floor areas. Merchandise was closely packed, but so were the shoppers who regarded the stores as no-nonsense, value-for-money retailers.

The easygoing relationship between Xou-Xou and her cousins had a favorable effect on the strong growth of the company. Although further shareholders had been admitted to the company, they were in the minority, and they did not inhibit board decisions. In addition to nonexecutive directors, the board had expanded to include a director responsible for finance and another person responsible for marketing and store development. Over the years, Xou-Xou had established a policy of selecting store managers from applicants with a good track record in buying and merchandising. She felt that she could partly attribute the success of her business to this.

Over the following 8 years, the company grew substantially; turnover grew from $9 million in 1995 to $71 million in 2003. The number of stores increased to 33, the majority of which were in Victoria, although six stores had been opened in two other states: four in New South Wales and two in South Australia. All the stores were located in suburban shopping centers. There were no plans to follow the lead of other retailers who were expanding into e-commerce and Internet shopping. One of the stated objectives of the company was, "*Aim for the middle market, avoiding the bottom segment, but getting low income groups trading up as well as upper income groups trading down.*" During this period, the company's product range also slightly expanded to include such related goods as electric shavers and hair dryers.

Contributions from shareholders, profit retentions, and suppliers' terms have financed the company's growth and operations; it never operated on an overdraft. Bank balances and cash-on-call amounted to $3.8 million of current assets in 2008. The relatively fast inventory turnover, absence of debtors, and reasonable creditor financing contribute to the company's positive cash flow. Toulette's Stores' cash flow enables Xou-Xou to meet her supplier commitments on time consistently, and she prides herself on the fact that she never misses a discount. She is loath to commit herself to long-term loans; additional long-term funding has always been obtainable from shareholders. Notwithstanding the introduction of new shareholders, control remains in the hands of Xou-Xou and her cousins.

Toulette's Stores: The Strategic Planning Process

We use this case to describe the strategic planning process in Toulette's Stores. Although Figure 2.1 outlines some key aspects of the strategic process, it does not indicate how Toulette's Stores (or any other organization) would progress through each stage of the process, in other words, the way in which it moves through the stages of building up to, and determining, strategies. With the exception of a one-person business, you need to ensure that members of the organization participate in each stage and agree substantially on the decisions made. There are several ways of approaching this process: one is the search conference, another is The Argenti System of Strategic Planning (The Argenti System); over a 40-year period, the cumulative number of users of this system exceeds 2,000.[21] Following The Argenti System, the CEO chairs a planning team of about seven top executives and a facilitator who guides the process. At stages that include SWOT analysis and strategy generation, the facilitator convenes larger groups with a broader membership. The involvement of the larger group draws on the embedded wisdom of the company and helps to achieve buy-in. While you do not have to employ the same approach, the underlying ideas of a team of executives, a facilitator, and broader participation and consultation may well be major contributors to success in this process. Another approach that builds participation in the process of developing strategies is the search conference, described in this chapter.

Management next needs to agree on what they wish to achieve, or what The Argenti System calls "the purpose objective" of the organization. Return on capital (ROC) is a suitable metric for this objective. Related to this is the statement of values, which recognizes responsibilities such as the welfare of employees. Toulette's Stores management is more likely to seek to earn a satisfactory return on capital than to maximize return.

Management now needs to quantify the return that they regard as satisfactory for the business. Based on the past performance and potential of Toulette's Stores, they agree on a target of 23% to be achieved over the next 5 years (see Table 2.3). Of course they need to recognize that this target is based on the current risk and return of the company, which may change if the fundamental nature of the business changes.

Table 2.2. Statement of values

Toulette's Stores	
Important stakeholders	**Values**
Management	Maintain effective management personnel
Employees	Be an equal opportunity employer
Customers	Keep prices low and offer value for money
Competitors	Keep up to date with and in front of competitors
Suppliers	Obtain optimum trading terms through effective, aggressive purchasing
Local community	Accept and meet the company's social responsibility
Government	Act with integrity and responsibility in its dealings with Government

Table 2.3. Forecast, target, and gap

Toulette's Stores	
Forecast ROC	17%
Target ROC	23%
GAP	6%

Having decided on the statement of values, specified the satisfactory return as a target of 23% ROC, and forecast the ROC as 17%, the gap of 6% clearly identifies the size of management's task. Following The Argenti System, the planning assistant for Toulette's Stores now calls separate meetings of a larger group of organizational members to identify strengths and weaknesses (internal analysis) and threats and opportunities (external analysis), respectively. By referring to a list of Functional areas, they may be able to add further items. At this point, participants do not label items as either strengths or weaknesses, as an item can sometimes be both a strength and a weakness. Table 2.4 shows the list after the planning team has added its views. Where appropriate, the planning team can refine this list by ranking the strengths and weaknesses (A, B, C) in terms of their strategic importance. Clearly, other functional areas feature according to the nature of the organization—production and research and development are examples.

While the approach to opportunities and threats is similar, participants also consider potential changes to existing items—locally, nationally, or globally (see Table 2.5). For example, given its niche market, Toulette's Stores may have few, if any, competitors, but new competitors may appear at any time, particularly as barriers to entry are relatively low (see Porter's five forces in this chapter).[22] The planning team can also refine this analysis by considering the potential impact of opportunities

Table 2.4. Strengths and weaknesses

Toulette's Stores	
Functional Area	**Strength or weakness**
Finance/legal	Strong cash resources, no debt, secure control
Marketing	Good image
Buying	Strong buying expertise
Employees	
Management	No successor
Position in Industry	Strong niche player, limited product range
Geographical	Strong in Victoria

Table 2.5. Threats and opportunities

Toulette's Stores	
Major area	**Threat or opportunity**
Competitive	Competitors
Political	
Economic	High unemployment, reduced disposable income, New South Wales market
Social	
Other	

and threats on the organization. The emergence of a strong competitor may have a significant impact, while reduced disposable income may leave toiletry sales relatively unscathed.

A group larger than the planning team is also useful for generating strategies. Brainstorming encourages creativity in suggesting strategies, and other techniques can extend the list of strategies. Table 2.6 shows the strategies for Toulette's Stores.

Management needs to evaluate the suggested strategies. One way to pare down this list is to see whether or not each strategy uses the organization's strengths, takes advantage of opportunities, reduces its weaknesses, or diminishes threats. Table 2.7 shows a sample of those strategies that fare reasonably well against these criteria. Following the table is a statement of the strategy the management of Toulette's Stores has adopted.

Table 2.6. Potential strategies

Toulette's Stores
Expand geographically, especially in New South Wales
Introduce house brands
Larger stores—expand floor areas
Diversify into wholesale "cash and carry"
Expand product range (liquor, food, furniture, clothing, jewelry, cut-price prescribed medicines)
Provide consumer credit (30-day accounts, revolving credit, 6 months to pay, store card, layaway)
Expand overseas
Mail order/Christmas club
Merger, acquisition, sale
Diversify into manufacturing
Introduce extensive training programs

Table 2.7. Evaluation of Strategies Against Criteria

Toulette's Stores		
	Positive impact on SWOT	**Negative impact on SWOT**
Expand geographically, especially in New South Wales (NSW)	Cash (S)	No successor (W)
	Good image (S)	Product range (W)
	Buying skills (S)	Control (S)
	Competitors (T)	
	NSW market (O)	
Introduce house brands	Good image (S)	Competitors (T)
	Buying skills (S)	NSW market (O)
	Competitors (T)	No successor (W)
	Cash (S)	Control (S)
Expand floor areas	Product range (W)	Control (S)
Expand product range	Cash (S)	Control (S)
	Buying skills (S)	
	Good image (S)	
	Product range (W)	
"Wholesale cash and carry"	Cash (S)	Skills shortage (T)
	Good image (S)	Control (S)
	Buying skills (S)	
	Product range (W)	

Toulette's Stores

Our Strategy

- We will open further stores in New South Wales, which we intend to equal our Victoria operations in size and profits within 7 years. We will not expand any further in Victoria.
- We will expand our product mix into food and electronics.
- We will diversify our traditional product/market sphere by establishing a mail order/Christmas club.
- We will introduce an in-house training program immediately, as skills shortages could seriously hinder our growth and diversification potential.
- To sustain our growth and reduce our vulnerability, we will develop a succession plan for top management.

Contemporary companies issue several statements concerning the way in which they do business. Three prominent statements are the vision statement, the mission statement, and the statement of values (see Table 2.1). These are dual-purpose statements—they govern the organization's operations and they inform stakeholders. The mission statement has three important elements—the products or services the organization provides, the customers it serves and the way in which it serves them. It may also feature the organization's main objective. For Toulette's Stores, after lengthy discussions, the members of the planning team agreed on the following vision statement: *"To become the leading retailer of value-for-money toiletries at low prices from no-frills premises for consumers in the middle segment of the market through applying our superior buying skills."* The planning team also agreed on the following mission statement: "*Our vision is to improve customers' lifestyles making value-for-money toiletries available at affordable prices.*"

While the statement of values provides reference points for navigating the strategic process, the planning team should craft the vision and the mission statements after the organization has decided on its strategy. Otherwise, they are preempting the strategic planning process.

CHAPTER 3

Pricing Strategies and Yield Management

Question: How do you choose which airline to fly with?
First passenger: I always travel on the same airline—so I can get lots of air miles.
Second passenger: I always travel on the same airline—because they have the best service.
Third passenger: I travel on whichever airline has the right combination of hubs and connecting flights at the right times—I hate having to transfer airlines and I hate having to wait for connecting flights.
Fourth passenger: I pick the airline that offers the cheapest price.

Businesses often fall in love with their products and services and overlook the reasons why customers buy them. The responses here show that customers can value different things, and what is most important to them is not always what you would expect. The value to the customer is a key factor in price setting and using yield management.

This chapter looks at the relationships between prices and yield management and how to develop strategies to maximize profits. Prices are the mechanism that allocates the supply of products and services among potential customers. Yield management is a technique that allocates capacity or inventory to products and services in order to maximize revenue. We view pricing and yield management as two sides of the same problem—*what volume of services should a business sell and at what price in order to maximize its profits?*

In the first part of this chapter, we examine the way businesses set prices and how they can implement demand-based pricing strategies to support yield management. In the second part, we discuss the technical aspects of implementing yield management and examine three popular approaches.

Pricing Tactics and Strategies

Prices are marketing variables that generate revenue. The price that a customer pays is revenue to the business and cost to the customer. This creates tension as businesses try to get the highest prices they can and customers try to get the lowest prices they can. This leads to a key concept in yield management—*willingness to pay*, that is, the maximum price each customer is willing to pay to acquire a product or service. If a customer can buy the product for less than the maximum price they are willing to pay, the difference is a *consumer surplus*. If they are unable to buy it at the price they want, this creates *unsatisfied customer demand*.

From the customer's perspective, the price also represents value for money. If the price is too high, the customer will not buy the product because they think they are not getting value for money. If the price is too low, this can also cause problems because the customer may use price as a signal of quality, and very low prices signal inferior quality. The trick is getting the price "just right."

A yield management strategy can incorporate multiple pricing strategies. These strategies should reflect the business's overall strategy. For example, we can consider pricing strategies in relation to Porter's generic categories[1] of product differentiation, cost leadership, or focus. Businesses following a product differentiation strategy or providing services based on value dimensions, such as the level of after-sales service, business location, or reputation, are likely to use a high-end pricing strategy. Businesses following a cost-leadership strategy are likely to use a low-end pricing strategy, where they try to build competitive advantage by maximizing the volume of sales through the use of bargain prices and minimal customer choice or support. Others following a focus strategy and competing on factors such as product availability, scope of services, and brand awareness are likely to price at the industry or market level.

Market Segmentation and Customer Characteristics

The first step in setting prices is to understand the characteristics of customers and the things they value about the products or services they purchase. Are they looking for convenience or low price? Are they prepared to pay extra for additional choices?

There are a variety of ways of segmenting customers into groups of people who have similar needs or wants using consumer demographics or lifestyles. One possible way of categorizing customers into groups based on price sensitivity is provided by Evans and Berman, and is as follows:[2]

- *Economic consumers.* Customers who want low prices and regard products or services as commodities.
- *Status-oriented consumers.* Customers who want prestige brands and a high level of customer service. They are prepared to pay higher prices and regard competing businesses as different.
- *Assortment-orientated consumers.* Customers who want a wide range of products and services to choose from, but they want to pay "fair" prices.
- *Personalizing consumers.* Customers who want to shop where employees know them and where they are attached to particular employees or stores. They will pay slightly higher prices than other customers.
- *Convenience-oriented consumers.* Customers who do not like shopping and who value convenience above other factors. They will pay higher prices. They want stores close to where they work or live, with long opening hours and the option to purchase remotely, such as through the Internet.

All businesses attract more than one type of customer. If a business is able to identify and segment their customers into homogeneous groups, they can potentially charge different prices to each segment. However, in general terms, if most of your customers are interested in low prices, then following a high-end pricing strategy is unlikely to be successful.

Setting Prices

A variety of ways exist to set prices in practice. These include using economic theory, cost-based pricing, and demand-based pricing. We consider how each of these can be used to follow a revenue management strategy. An obvious solution to the pricing problem is to use market prices. However, for many products or services, there may be no reliable comparison price in the market. This could be because a product is new, it is thinly traded, it has no direct competition, or it is continually subject to development and improvement. In such instances, an alternative method to the market price must be found in order to set prices.

A quick word about monopolies, oligopolies, and cartels—if a business controls the market and demand exceeds supply, then it can potentially charge what it likes and maximize revenue by selling as much as possible at the highest prices. This is subject, of course, to regulations governing monopoly pricing, any political costs, and the threat of new entrants to the market. In this chapter, we deal with the more common situation where competition exists, with many sellers and many buyers.

Economic-Based Pricing

Classical economic theory provides that as price increases, customer demand decreases. However, different market conditions lead to different relationships between price and quantity sold, reflecting different consumer price sensitivities.

Figure 3.1 illustrates the market demand and supply curve. The market demand curve (D) represents the willingness to pay of customers for particular products or services. The market supply curve (*S*) represents the quantity (*Q*) of product or services all firms in the market are willing

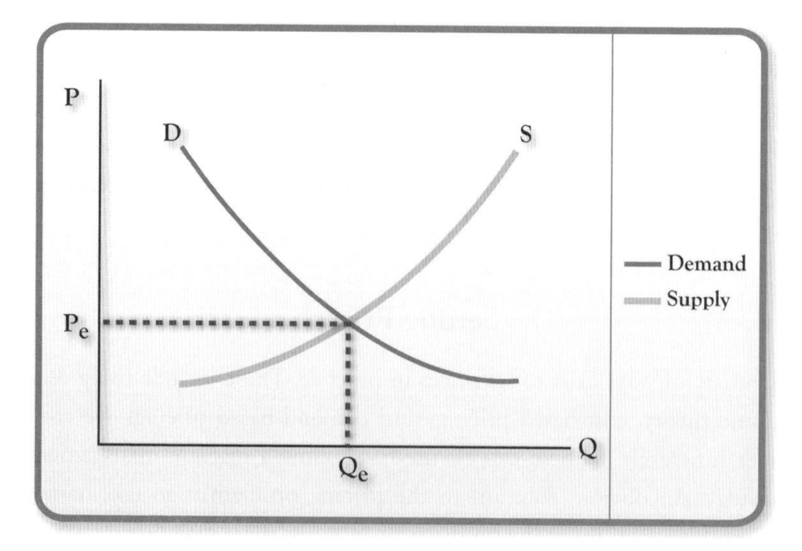

Figure 3.1. Market demand and supply curve

to supply at different prices (*P*). Generally, as marginal costs increase or marginal revenue decreases, the quantity of goods or services that firms are willing to supply to the marketplace will reduce. Equilibrium in the market occurs at the price-quantity (*Pe*/*Qe*) combination, where the market demand and supply curves intersect.

An individual firm maximizes its profits where its marginal revenue equals its marginal cost of production. Under perfect competition, this will also be where the price equals marginal revenue and marginal cost. If a business is acting rationally in setting its prices, under economic theory it needs to know its marginal revenue and its marginal costs. A reasonable estimate of the marginal cost should be available to the business. This marginal cost will equal either the cost of making an additional unit of product or the cost of providing an additional service. However, estimating marginal revenue requires information on the price-demand relationship for the particular product or service. Practically, this is difficult. This information could be identified through surveys (asking customers whether they would buy the product at particular prices) or by observing changes in demand directly where different prices are changed either over time or in different markets.

This approach appears to provide a simple approach to pricing that maximizes a business's revenue in a single-price market. In practice, difficulties with the estimation of marginal revenue may prevent its use and leads to many businesses using cost-based pricing. Further, the charging of a single price by a business means there will be a consumer surplus. That is, some customers will pay less than they are willing to pay. If a business could charge multiple prices, then it would be able to tap into this consumer surplus, thereby increasing its revenue.

Cost-Based Pricing

It is a truism that every viable business must be able to earn revenue in excess of its total costs. In practice, there can be periods when prices are less than cost due to market penetration strategies, stock management policies, or economic conditions. However, such practices are not sustainable in the long run. This focus on profit encourages many businesses to use some form of cost-plus pricing, which explicitly sets prices in terms of cost and profit.

We can use several approaches, starting with different estimates of the unit cost. Unit cost can be specified in terms of variable cost, manufacturing cost (which includes variable manufacturing costs and an allocation of fixed manufacturing costs), or total cost (which includes manufacturing costs and an allocation of selling, general, and administrative costs). In each case, the target profit added will vary depending on whether it needs to cover other costs in the business not included in the unit cost estimate. The target profit also needs to cover the business's opportunity cost of funds and its competitive and risk positions.

The following example illustrates how a business could set prices using its variable cost plus a target profit. Table 3.1 provides relevant data for a small boutique hotel. Using the information on the expected number of rooms occupied in the year (21,900 room nights), the variable costs ($50), other costs ($715,000) and the target profit

Table 3.1. Example Hotel Cost-Plus Pricing

Relevant Revenue and Cost Data	
Number of hotel rooms	75
Expected average occupancy rate	80%
Expected annual room occupancy (75 rooms × 365 nights × 80%)	21,900
Hotel investment value	$7,500,000
Desired return on investment (before tax)	15%
Estimated variable costs per room per night	$50
Administration	$125,000
Selling	$100,000
Depreciation	$200,000
Insurance	$95,000
Utilities	$120,000
Repairs and maintenance	$75,000
Estimated annual fixed costs	$715,000
Calculation	
Required profit before tax ($7.5 million × 15%)	$1,125,000
Plus annual fixed costs	$715,000
Required operating income	$1,840,000
Estimated variable costs (21,900 × $50)	$1,095,000
Required revenue	$2,935,000
Required revenue per room night ($2,935,000/21,900 room nights)	$134.02

($1,125,000), a hotel room rate of $135 (rounded) can be calculated using this approach.

This approach is intuitively appealing, as it both covers the business's costs and also targets the owner's required return on their investment. However, there are a number of problems with this approach. The most important arises where there is a ready price for a competing service. If the price charged by the business is higher than the competition's price, then it will struggle to find customers and its capacity utilization rate will go down. Using the cost-plus method, this, in turn, would encourage the business to put its prices up, which will just makes things worse. Similarly, if the business is charging less than its competitors using cost-based pricing, then it will be sacrificing revenue it might otherwise earn.

Even if the problems with the market price are overcome, further difficulties can arise with calculating the price. Our example is deliberately simple, with one room type and one rate for the whole year. In reality, such a business is likely to have different room types, charge different prices in the high and low seasons, and charge different prices to different types of customers. Once these (and more) complications are incorporated into the calculation, this method becomes much less appealing.

Demand-Based (Strategic) Pricing

Marketers have always known that in a competitive environment, if you charge a price that is significantly different from your competitors', then you will not be able to sell anything unless you can differentiate your product. However, the flip side is that the price of differentiated products can be set at a level that reflects the value that customers place on the product or service. If this is possible, the relationship between the price of your product and the cost of production or your competitors' prices is less important. Using demand-based pricing provides businesses with the opportunity to generate the maximum revenue from their customer base, as prices are closely linked to customers' willingness to pay. This willingness often has little connection to the underlying costs.

Technology companies, for example, have long recognized that their customers can be broadly divided into market segments comprising early adopters, who are prepared to pay a high price to obtain the latest technology; late adopters, who will only acquire new technology when the price is low enough; and the rest, whose desire to acquire new technology falls somewhere between the two extremes. (We note that, in reality, there are likely to be more than three separable groups of consumers for many technology products.) Accordingly, the cost of new technology is not the primary driver of pricing patterns over time, but rather the willingness of different groups to acquire that technology at different prices. Prices are set at high levels, initially, to capture the maximum revenue from early adopters; next, the price is lowered to a medium level to attract the next group of adopters; and, finally, when the technology is no longer cutting-edge, prices are set at a low level to sell to the late adopters. This strategy allows companies to charge prices that mirror their customers' willingness to pay.

This strategic approach to pricing requires businesses to identify the value of their product to different customer segments and then communicate that value to the different segments. Problems arise when businesses fail to communicate the value and customers feel they are not getting value for money. This failure can occur where pricing schemes are complicated, where they frequently change, or where they are not linked to what customers value. Examples of these types of failures can be seen with many utilities, such as telecommunications and electricity suppliers. Customers can be confused over what they are paying for and the reasons for differences between pricing plans. Further, where pricing plans change frequently, customers are left feeling like they have paid too much. The failure to link the price of these services to the value to the customer leads to customer discontent over pricing and to switching between suppliers.

Berry and Yadav[3] identify three demand-based pricing strategies service businesses can use to overcome these problems and to better communicate value to customers. The pricing of services is particularly difficult given the intangible nature of the benefits received by the customer. In particular, customers are not able to "test-drive" a service in the same way they can with a tangible product and so do not necessarily know what they are getting or how good it might be.

The first strategy suggested by Berry and Yadav[4] is *satisfaction-based pricing.* This strategy includes service guarantees, flat-rate pricing, and benefit-driven pricing. Service guarantees and flat-rate pricing reduce customer risk by guaranteeing either the service quality or the price. Benefit-driven pricing explicitly links the pricing mechanism to the features of the service that the customer values. For example, Internet connection fees are charged based on the information downloaded rather than the time spent using the service, as it is the use made of the service that customers value, not the time.

The second strategy, *relationship-based pricing*, links customer value to the price by building longer-term relationships between customers and businesses using either long-term contracts or price bundling. These longer-term relationships generate efficiencies that can be shared between the customer and the business. Long-term contracts create a more regular relationship between the customer and supplier. Price bundling, where multiple products or services are sold together, generates additional business from existing customers. An example of price bundling is travel companies that offer "all-inclusive" pricing packages. Customers feel that they are getting better value for the prices they pay, and businesses are able to gain cost efficiencies from supplying multiple services to single customers.

The third strategy, *efficiency pricing*, links customer value to the price by using cost-leadership strategies to manage the costs of the business and then pass those cost savings to the customers. For example, low-cost commuter airlines have streamlined their operations so that their prices only cover services that most customers value, such as a seat on the plane, and provide surcharges for the parts they do not value, such as additional baggage allowance and meals (remember Southwest Airlines in Chapter 2, which did not provide in-flight meals).

The purpose of all three approaches is to link the price of the product or service to the value to the customer. Often, businesses think of prices in terms of their cost of supply, whereas the customer considers the price in terms of the value they receive. If a business can change its pricing strategy from a cost focus to a customer-value focus, then it will be able to better implement the yield management techniques discussed in the next part of this chapter.

Yield Management

The goal of yield management is to charge each customer a price equal to the highest price they are willing to pay. In this way, a business can maximize revenue from its available capacity. While some argue yield management can be implemented by any business, more generally, the following characteristics[5] have been identified as present in businesses that benefit the most from yield management:

- The existence of *fixed capacity*, which is unable to be changed quickly to meet changes in demand. These types of businesses incur high costs to increase or decrease capacity but have low marginal costs (e.g., if a hotel sells an empty room to a customer, the associated marginal costs are relatively low, but to increase the number of rooms in the hotel is expensive and time consuming).
- The ability to *segment customers*, where different customer groups have different levels of willingness to pay for products or services.
- The existence of *fluctuating demand*, where demand fluctuates widely between seasons, days of the week, time of the day, or due to other factors.
- The existence of *perishable inventory*, where inventory or capacity that is unsold at the time of production cannot be stored and used later (e.g., empty seats on an aircraft cannot be sold once the scheduled flight has departed).
- *Product sold in advance*, where businesses have to choose between taking a booking now at a lower price versus holding the inventory or capacity in the expectation that a higher price can be obtained (e.g., for a rental car business, it is the choice between selling a discounted rental car reservation now or waiting until close to the reservation date and selling the reservation at a higher price).

Sorting Mechanisms and Rate Fences

Yield management sets prices based on the value customer segments place on the products or services supplied by the business, that is, it uses demand-based pricing. In practice, this requires the segmentation of customers into groups using a *sorting mechanism*. Sorting mechanisms need to be meaningful to customers. For example, sorting customers into men and women is unlikely to be relevant for hotel rooms, as each group is likely to have a similar willingness to pay. In contrast, sorting customers by gender is likely to be relevant for hairdressing, as women will be more willing to pay higher prices.

Customer segments also need to be capable of being kept separate to ensure that customers prepared to pay high prices are not converted into customers who pay low prices. For example, a hotel's customers might consist of business customers with a high willingness to pay and holiday travelers with a low willingness to pay. In order to keep these two groups separate and to discourage business customers from paying lower prices, *rate fences* are needed. Rate fences can be either physical and affect the nature of what is supplied or nonphysical and act as restrictions on usage. For example, a hotel might provide rooms with better views to the customers who pay the higher room rate (physical fence) or they might require that customers paying the lower price have to stay on a Saturday night (nonphysical fence). Many different types of rate fences are used in practice. Examples of physical rate fences include

- type of product or service supplied (e.g., in a restaurant, higher prices might be charged for tables located by the window);
- the amenities provided (e.g., an economy airfare may vary depending on whether a customer has hand luggage only or also has check-in luggage).

Examples of nonphysical rate fences include

- time of reservation (e.g., advanced purchase or spot purchase);
- time of usage restrictions (e.g., day of week, season, or time of day);
- purchase restrictions (e.g., cancellation options or alteration options);
- purchase volume restrictions (e.g., group versus individual bookings);
- duration of usage (e.g., length of stay or usage);
- group membership.

In practice, the creation of rate fences is part art and part science. Importantly, the fences used must be meaningful to customers and they must keep different customer segments separate. For example, consider a small airline that operates a five-seater aircraft from San Jose to Seattle and has identified five potential customers. The maximum price each customer is willing to pay is shown in Table 3.2.

If our airline could sell every seat on every flight at the customers' maximum price, the total revenue per flight would be $895. Alternatively,

Table 3.2. Airline Example: Customers' Willingness to Pay

Customer	Price
A	$280
B	$250
C	$170
D	$145
E	$50
Total	$895

if the airline charges a single fare, then the total revenue will vary depending on the price, as shown in Table 3.3. If the price is $280, then only Customer A will purchase a ticket. If the price is $50, then all the customers will purchase a ticket. Using a single fare, the price that will maximize revenue will be $145, which gives us total revenue of $580 per flight. This is only 64.8% of the possible maximum of $895.

However, if we identify rate fences that can effectively segregate our customers, then we can get closer to the theoretical maximum of $895. Using the data from Table 3.2, we can segment customers into *full-fare customers* (A and B), *discount-fare customers* (C and D), and *deep-discount customers* (E).

Our airline has identified that full-fare customers want to retain complete flexibility over the purchase of their tickets, without penalty. In contrast, discount-fare customers are prepared to purchase their tickets in advance and pay a penalty if they need to change their bookings, but only if the price is lower than the full fare. Finally, deep-discount customers are prepared to fly on "standby" tickets and will accept being "bumped" from flights, provided they only have to pay very low prices. In this way, we have created three distinct products from one service, as shown in Table 3.4 with the flight from San Jose to Seattle.

Table 3.3. Airline Example: Single Fare

Fare charged ($)	Fare paid by each customer ($)					Total revenue ($)
	Customer A	Customer B	Customer C	Customer D	Customer E	
280	280	0	0	0	0	280
250	250	250	0	0	0	500
170	170	170	170	0	0	510
145	145	145	145	145	0	580
50	50	50	50	50	50	250

Table 3.4. Airline example—fare classes

Fare Class	Price	Advance purchase	Penalty for booking changes	Standby	Customers
Full-fare	$250	No	No	No	A, B
Discount	$145	Yes	Yes	No	C, D
Deep-discount	$50	Yes	Yes	Yes	E

With these three new products (full-fare, discount, and deep-discount tickets), we can now recalculate the total revenue, which will be $840 with 100% utilization (all seats are sold), as shown in Table 3.5. This is 93.9% of our theoretical maximum, a significant improvement from using a single fare (as shown in Table 3.3).

How Do You Identify a Customer's Willingness to Pay?

In our airline example, each customer's willingness to pay was given. In practice, we are unlikely to know this information as precisely. Instead, estimates for customer segments have to be determined based on the available information. Ways of identifying this information include market surveys, past data on prices, and prices in geographically distinct markets.

There are businesses where customers' willingness to pay can be observed directly. These exceptions usually relate to situations where customers are competitively bidding for products or services, such as auctions. The *Dutch Auction* provides a real-world example where willingness to pay can be measured directly. In these auctions, the price starts high and is gradually reduced by the auctioneer until bidders enter the market. Accordingly, potential customers are encouraged to pay the highest price they are willing to pay. A similar example is closed tenders, where prospective buyers must provide their best bid for the property for sale, often real estate, without knowing what others are bidding. Again,

Table 3.5. Airline example—multiple fares

Fare charged ($)	Fare Paid by Each Customer ($)					Total Revenue ($)
	Customer A	Customer B	Customer C	Customer D	Customer E	
250; 145 and 50	250	250	145	145	50	840

this encourages buyers to offer the highest price they are prepared to pay. However, in most businesses, auctions or tenders are not a practical way of selling products or services. As such, willingness to pay must be estimated based on available information.

Allocation of Inventory and Forecasting Demand

In our airline example, it was relatively easy to allocate the seating capacity (inventory) to each customer segment (or *price or rate class),* as there were only three rate classes and the total capacity was five seats per flight. In practice, the problem of allocating inventory or capacity to each rate class is more complex. The degree of difficulty associated with making these allocations will determine the complexity of the yield management method needed to ensure revenue is maximized.

If there is infinite demand for all rate classes, then revenue is maximized by selling all inventory at the highest price. However, usually there is limited demand for high prices and excess demand for low prices. Accordingly, businesses need to allocate inventory to each rate class in such a way that total revenue is maximized.

Complicating this problem is the issue of forecasting when each customer will make his or her purchase. If a business sells all of its inventory at the lowest price, then there will be none left to sell to customers prepared to pay higher prices. Businesses have to trade off an immediate sale to a low-price customer against the possibility of a future sale to a high-price customer.

This allocation process requires us to forecast demand over the *booking period* so we can determine whether to sell now or hold capacity for high-price customers. The booking period is the period of time between when bookings open to the day that the inventory or capacity is provided to the customer. For example, for the sale of a hotel room, the booking period could be 12 months before the customer uses the hotel room.

The yield management methods available to businesses each involve forecasting customer demand and allocating inventory to different rate classes, but the extent of the data required and complexity of the allocation method vary. We consider three methods. The simplest is the *threshold curve* method, next is the *expected marginal seat revenue* (EMSR) method, and the most complex involves *linear programming.*

Threshold Curves

Threshold curves are relatively easy to use and are popular in businesses such as hotels and rental car businesses. Threshold curves provide a method of determining whether to (a) open discount-price classes to encourage demand, when customer demand is lower than expected, or (b) close discount-price classes to ensure capacity is allocated to high-price customers, when customer demand is higher than expected.

Figure 3.2 shows a threshold curve, where bookings or reservations for a service to be provided on a particular date (Day 0) are tracked over the booking period (in this case 90 days before Day 0). The forecast relates to a season or specific date that the service is to be provided (e.g., the Fourth of July or the summer season) and the horizontal axis shows the number of days before the commencement date. The solid, wavy line shows actual bookings over the booking period and the broken lines show the upper and lower limits set by management. At 90 days before Day 0, bookings are low, but they increase as the period gets closer to the date when the service will be provided to the customer. When actual bookings on a particular day or week (or other review period) are above the upper limit, one or more discount-price classes will be closed. When bookings are less than expected and drop below the lower limit, one or more discount-price classes will be opened.

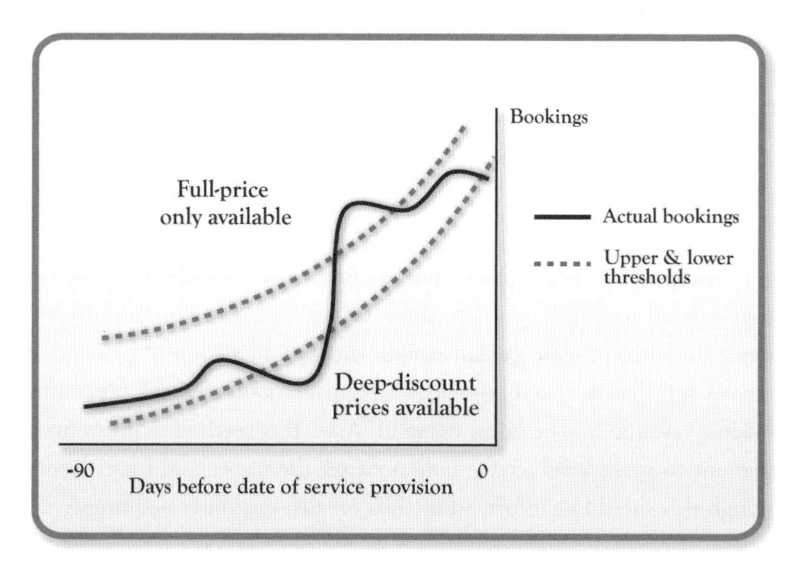

Figure 3.2. Threshold curve

To implement a threshold curve system, the following conditions and information are necessary:

- There must be a booking period before the date of service provision where predictions about expected customer demand by rate class can be made.
- There must be multiple rate classes that can be opened and closed in response to actual customer bookings over the booking period.
- There must be data on past bookings by day and rate class, possibly also reflecting different booking levels for different times during the year (i.e., incorporating seasonal effects). These data are used to set the upper and lower limits for expected customer demand.
- Actual bookings must be frequently monitored against the upper and lower limits of expected demand to determine whether the combination of rate classes available to customers needs to be altered.

The business needs to apply the following decision rule on a regular basis to ensure the revenue generated from actual bookings approximates maximum revenue:

- *If bookings are less than expected (below the lower limit), open the lowest price classes.*
- *If bookings are more than expected (above the upper limit), close the lowest price classes.*

This approach is relatively simple and is used widely as it appears to give good results. The main disadvantage with the *threshold curve* is that it does not provide guidance as to the best allocation of demand to rate classes, that is, it only provides an approximation of the maximum possible revenue for the given demand. Also, this method requires management to make a subjective judgment on the upper and lower limits, though this should be informed by data on past customer bookings.

Expected Marginal Seat Revenue (EMSR)

A more sophisticated method of identifying the optimal combinations of rate classes to sell to customers is provided by the *expected marginal seat revenue* (EMSR) method. This method was developed in the airline industry (hence, the "seat" in EMSR started life as an aircraft seat) and was first described by Littlewood.[6] However, the approach can be used in any business where there is a sufficiently sophisticated booking system and predictable patterns of customer demand. The essence of this method is that it trades off the revenue from selling a discounted fare now against the expected revenue from selling a seat at a higher fare later.

For example, say an aircraft has a capacity of 180 seats for a particular sector. Seats are available for sale either at a full fare (P_h) of $450 or at a discount fare (P_d) of $200. The airline management would like to sell all the seats on each sector at the full fare, but past bookings show that this is not achievable for most of the year. The airline has received a booking request 1 month in advance for a seat at the discount fare of $200. Should the airline accept the booking at the lower fare or wait in the hope that a customer prepared to pay the higher fare will book in the future? If the booking is rejected, there is the possibility that the seat will be unoccupied when the aircraft departs. If the booking is accepted, there is the possibility that the airline will have to turn down a booking at the higher fare of $450.

Assume that 1 month before the booking date the airline knows that there are still some customers who will book and pay for a seat at the higher price, but there is only a 30% probability of this happening. The EMSR from holding on to this seat is therefore $450 × 30%, which equals $135. As the airline has just received a booking from a customer willing to pay the discount rate of $200 now, the better decision is to accept the discount customer's offer. More formally, the relationship between the EMSR for high prices and lower prices is illustrated in Figure 3.3.

Figure 3.3 shows the expected revenue from selling one more seat (*X1*), where S seats have been sold already for that fare class. This line represents the following formula:

$$\text{EMSR} = \text{P}_h \times \Pr(X_1 \geq S)$$

For the full-fare tickets, the airline knows it can sell at least 20 seats (probability [*Pr*] of an additional sale is 100%), so the EMSR for selling another

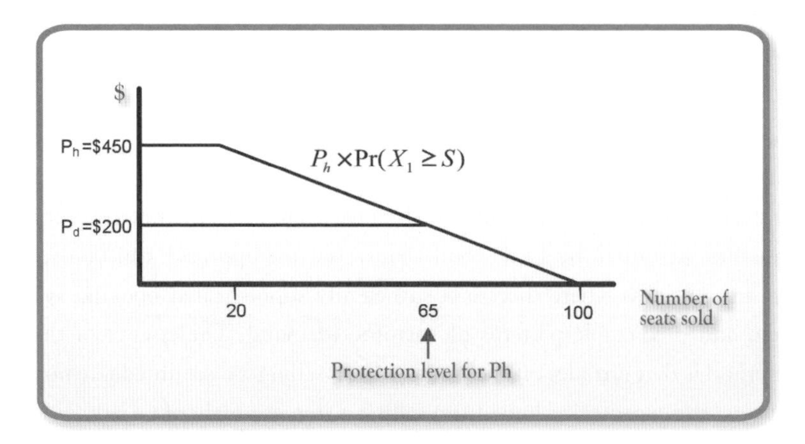

Figure 3.3. Expected marginal revenue for full-fare and discount-fare tickets

seat up to 20 seats is $450. It also knows that it is unable to sell more than 100 seats (probability of an additional sale is 0%), so the EMSR is $0. Between 20 and 100, the probability of selling an additional seat is uniformly distributed, with a mean of 60 seats (= 20 + (100–20)/2). Accordingly, the EMSR declines from $450 (for 20 seats) to $0 (for 100 seats). The airline also knows it can sell all of the aircraft's capacity at the discount fare. That is, the probability of selling an additional seat at the discount fare is 100% and the EMSR for the discount fare is $200 for all seats available to sell. The point where the two lines intersect is where the EMSR for the full-fare ticket equals the EMSR for the discount ticket, that is, $200. This intersection point can be found when 65 full-fare seats have been sold.

Where do the numbers come from? To determine the number of seats to reserve for P_h, the airline needs to find the intersection point where the EMSR for P_h equals the EMSR for P_d, that is, $200. Beyond this level, the EMSR for P_h is less than P_d, and the airline should sell the seats at the discount fare now, rather than wait for a full-fare customer to make a booking in the future. This is illustrated in Table 3.6. This table shows the cumulative probability that demand will be less than a particular number of seats, *F(Q)*, and the probability of selling one more seat once a particular number of seats has already been sold, *Pr(X1* ≥ S). For example, there is a cumulative probability of 56.25%

that demand will be less than 65 full-fare seats. Therefore, the probability of selling one more seat is 43.75%. This means the EMSR for selling one more seat once 65 have been sold is $197 (= 43.75% × $450). This is approximately equal to the discount fare of $200.

The cumulative probability at the intersection point for the EMSR for the two fare classes shown in Table 3.6 can be directly calculated using the following formula:

$$F(Q) \geq \frac{(P_h - P_d)}{P_h}$$

where $F(Q) = Pr(X_1 < S)$ is the cumulative probability that demand for P_h will be less than the protection level (S). In our example, $F(Q) = 55.6\% = (450–200)/450$. This is approximately at the level of 65 seats, shown in Table 3.6.

Using the information from Table 3.6, the airline should have a *protection level* of 65 seats for full-fare passengers and book up to (but no more than) 115 seats for the discount-fare passengers. This is the *booking limit* for the discount fare and is equal to total capacity (180 seats) minus the protection level for the full fare as shown in Figure 3.4.

Table 3.6. Example EMSR Calculation

Number of		**Full-Fare (P_h) $450**		**Discount Fare (P_d) $200**	
seats sold (S)	$F(Q)$	**Pr(X_1≥S) P_h**	**EMSRP_h**	**Pr(X_1≥S)P_d**	**EMSRP_d**
15	0.00%	100.00%	$450	100%	$200
20	0.00%	100.00%	$450	100%	$200
30	12.50%	87.50%	$394	100%	$200
40	25.00%	75.00%	$338	100%	$200
50	37.50%	62.50%	$281	100%	$200
60	50.00%	50.00%	$225	100%	$200
65	56.25%	43.75%	$197	100%	$200
70	62.50%	37.50%	$169	100%	$200
80	75.00%	25.00%	$113	100%	$200
90	87.50%	12.50%	$56	100%	$200
100	100.00%	0.00%	$0	100%	$200

Note: $Pr(X_1 \geq S) = 1 - F(Q)$

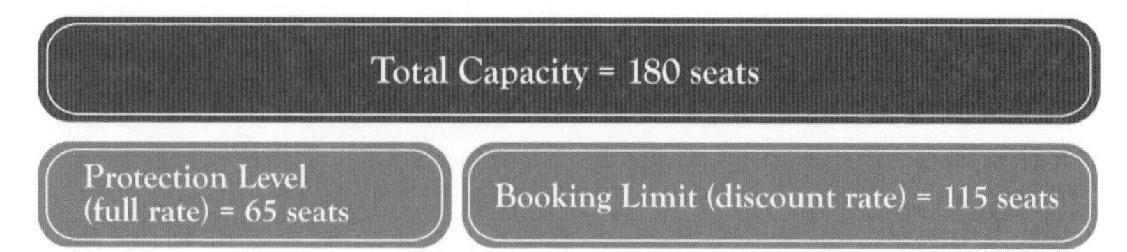

Figure 3.4 Relationship between booking limits and protection levels

In our example, the cumulative probability distribution for customer demand is uniformly distributed. More commonly, businesses will use a normal or Poisson distribution to model customer demand, or, if sufficient data are available, an empirical distribution based on past customer demand could be used.

The calculation of protection levels and booking limits allows a business to allocate capacity to different fare classes in a way that generates, approximately, the maximum total revenue for the number of fare classes and expected demand. However, the EMSR method is only a "rule of thumb," that is, the allocations only approach optimal levels. It is possible that another combination of fare allocations could provide a slightly better level of revenue. However, compared to the *threshold curve* method, which is also a "rule of thumb," the EMSR provides a better approximation of the optimal level.

Overbooking

Service businesses with booking systems, such as airlines, hotels, and restaurants, are very aware of the problem of customers booking but not showing up. These businesses have fixed capacity and these *no-shows* result in wasted capacity, for example, the empty airline seat on the flight from New York to Boston. Businesses can encourage customers to contact them if they are not going to use their booking through the use of penalties. But this approach only partly addresses the problem of lost revenue and wasted capacity. This problem can be particularly frustrating for businesses when the wasted capacity could have been resold to customers wanting the booking, for example, empty tables in restaurants where there is a queue of customers waiting to be seated.

If you can accurately estimate the number of customers who will be "no-shows," overbooking provides a solution to this problem. Anyone who flies regularly will be familiar with the idea of overbooking. For example, if an airline has capacity on a particular sector of 180 seats and it knows from experience that 10% of customers will be no-shows, then it can book up to 200 seats on the basis that only 180 passengers are likely to check in. Otherwise, if the airline books only 180 seats and only 162 passengers check in, then the aircraft will depart with 18 empty seats. These empty seats represent a cost to the airline in terms of lost revenue.

But what happens if the airline books 200 seats and 190 passengers attempt to check in? This is what airlines dread—a passenger with a ticket, but no seat available. In our example, there will be 10 passengers who have missed their flight and the airline will incur a variety of costs to provide compensation. These costs can take the form of financial penalties payable to the customer or to another customer willing to give up their seat for that flight, costs related to finding alternative flights or alternative seats on the aircraft (upgrade costs), and hotel or meal costs while the customer waits for the next flight. In addition, there will be nonfinancial costs related to the loss of customer goodwill and the loss of business reputation. No airline can afford to have a reputation for "bumping" passengers. These nonfinancial costs are often underestimated but, in the longer term, can have a more significant impact than the immediate financial costs.

Determining the optimal number of seats (or rooms or other service unit) to overbook requires a trade-off between the expected costs (C) and the expected benefits (B) of overbooking. The benefits are the *lost revenue* from the empty seat, that is, the benefit that could have been obtained if the empty seat had been overbooked. The costs are any penalties from overbooking. The net benefit or cost will be determined by the actual number of no-shows (X) compared to the actual number of seats overbooked (Y). To calculate the optimal number of seats to overbook, (Y^*), you need to know the distribution of the number of no-shows. Using this information, you can calculate the expected costs and compare those to the expected benefits. If the expected benefits exceed the expected costs of overbooking one more seat, then the business should do so. If the expected costs are more than the expected benefits, then no further overbooking should be accepted.

Where do the numbers come from? You can calculate the optimal number of seats to overbook (Y^*) by using the following formula, where $F(Y)$ is the distribution of the number of no-shows.

$$F(Y^*) \geq \frac{B}{(B+C)}$$

So in our airline example, where the aircraft capacity is 180 seats, we know that the lost revenue is $200 per seat and the penalty costs for bumping passengers are $300 per passenger. If we overbook 20 seats and $X = 22$ (the actual number of no-shows), then the lost revenue (B) is $400 (two empty seats at $200 per seat). If $X = 18$, then the penalty is $600 (two passengers bumped from the flight at $300 per person).

Using this formula, the factor for $F(Y^*)$ is 0.40. Assuming the distribution of the no-shows, $F(Y)$ is normally distributed with a mean of 20 and a standard deviation of 5, we can use the normal distribution to calculate the optimal number of no-shows. Using either normal distribution tables or software statistical functions, the answer is 18.73 seats. As we cannot overbook 0.73 of a seat, we should round this up to 19 seats or down to 18 seats. This is the number of seats we should overbook.

Nested EMSR (Multiple Rate Classes)

The existence of multiple customer segments allows businesses to develop multiple products with multiple prices from, essentially, a single product or service. In our EMSR airline example, we had two different price classes—a full-fare and a discount-fare ticket. These two prices are *distinct or nested classes,* where the sum of inventory or capacity allocated to each class must equal total capacity (or if overbooking is allowed, total capacity plus the amount of overbooking). The formula we used only provided for two rate classes, but, in practice, there are likely to be many rate classes. The EMSR formula can be modified to calculate protection levels and booking limits for any number of fare classes.

To use EMSR for multiple fare classes, it is necessary to use weighted average prices to calculate the combined protection levels. This is illustrated in Figure 3.5 using an example of a hotel with 500 rooms and four different room rates. From the highest to lowest price, these are the rack rate, corporate rate,

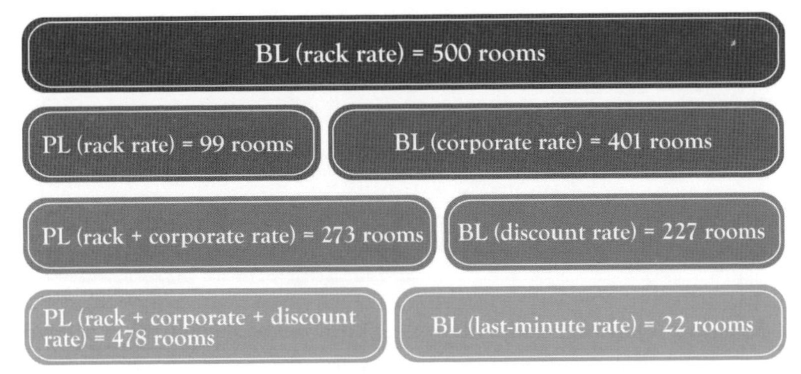

Figure 3.5. Nested protection levels (PL) and booking limits (BL)

discount rate, and the last-minute rate. Figure 3.5 illustrates two important issues when making these calculations. First, the booking limit and protection level for each level cannot exceed total capacity. Second, for each protection level, the total protection is for that fare class and all higher-fare classes.

Where do the numbers come from? The formula for calculating the EMSR where there are multiple rate classes is modified to allow for *n* rate classes where *fi* is the rate for the *i*th class. For each fare class, we have an expected level of demand with a corresponding variance:

n = number of fare classes

fi = revenue for fare class I, where $f1 \geq f2 \geq \ldots \geq fn$

μi = mean demand of fare class i

σ_i^2 = variance of demand of fare class i

PLi = protection level of fare classes i and higher

A weighted average fare is calculated for each fare level we are protecting and any fare levels above. For example, if calculating the protection level for the corporate rate, we would calculate the weighted average fare for the rack rate and corporate rate together. The weighted average is calculated as follows, where j denotes the levels above i. If $i = 3$, then j would denote levels 1 and 2.

$$f_{i+1} = \bar{f}_i P(D_i > \theta_i)$$

where . . .

$$\bar{f}_i = \frac{\sum_{j=1}^{i} \mu_j f_j}{\sum_{j=1}^{i} \mu_i}$$

$$D_i \sim \text{Normal with mean } \sum_{j=1}^{i} \mu_i \text{ and variance } \sum_{j=1}^{i} \sigma^2$$

Assuming a normal distribution is applicable (note that other theoretical distributions may better describe the distribution for particular real world examples), the z_α in the following refers to the number of standard deviations in the normal distribution.

$$\Rightarrow PL_i = \mu_i + z_\alpha \sigma_i, \quad \text{where } F(z_\alpha) = 1 - \frac{f_{i+1}}{\bar{f}_i}$$

Note that *1 – fi+1 / fi* is the same as our previous formula where there were only two fares, $(P_h - P_d) / P_h$. The only differences for nested EMSRs are that there are more than two fare classes and the denominator is the weighted average fare.

Using our hotel example, the relevant calculations illustrated in Figure 3.5 are provided in Table 3.7. The top half of Table 3.7 shows the prices for each fare class and the associated mean, variation, and standard deviation of the demand for each fare class. These data are used in the bottom half of Table 3.7 to calculate the numbers needed for the nested EMSR formulas. For fare class 1, *F1* (the rack rate only), the aggregated data are the same for both. For fare class 2, *F2* (the rack rate and the corporate rate together), the weighted average fare is calculated as [($150×100) + ($100×175)]/(100+175) = $118. For fare class 3, *F3* (the rack rate, the corporate rate, and the discount rate together), the weighted average fare is calculated as [($150×100) + ($100×175) + ($75×200)]/(100 + 175 + 200) = $100. The aggregate mean demand and variance are calculated by aggregating the respective figures in each column. For example, for fare class 3, the aggregated mean is 100 + 175 + 200 = 475 and 10 + 12 + 15 = 37 for the aggregated variance. Note that we cannot aggregate the standard deviation the same way but have to calculate them using the variance. Notice also that we do not calculate the weighted average fare for

F4; this is because the last-minute rate is the lowest fare class and we do not need to protect capacity for this last class.

The nested EMSR calculations for each level are then calculated as follows (this is illustrated in Figure 3.5). For the first level (*F1*), $F(Z_\alpha)$ = 1 – (100/150) = 0.333. From the normal distribution, this is –0.43 standard deviations. Accordingly, the protection level (for the rack rate) is set as *PL1* = 100 – (0.43×3.16) = 99 rooms (rounded), and the booking limit (for the corporate rate) for level *F1* is 500 – 99 = 401 rooms.

For the second level (*F2*), $F(Z_\alpha)$ = 1 – (75/118) = 0.364. From the normal distribution, this is –0.35 standard deviations. Accordingly, the protection level (for the rack rate and corporate rate together) is set as *PL2* = 275 – (0.35×4.69) = 273 rooms (rounded) and the booking limit (for the discount rate) for level *F2* is 500 – 273 = 227 rooms.

For the third level (*F3*), $F(Z_\alpha)$ = 1 – (30/100) = 0.70. From the normal distribution, this is +0.53 standard deviations. Accordingly, the protection level (for the rack rate, corporate rate, and discount rate together) is set as *PL3* = 475 + (0.53×6.08) = 478 rooms (rounded) and the booking limit (for the last-minute rate) for Level *F3* is 500 – 478 = 22 rooms.

While EMSR is a useful tool for estimating maximum revenue, there are more sophisticated models available that calculate combinations of fares and capacity allocations that will provide better approximations of the optimum revenue. Regardless, EMSR, in both its simplified and nested versions, remains one of the most widely used methods.

Table 3.7. Nested EMSR Example

		Demand		
Fare class	**Fare rate**	**Mean**	**Variance**	**Std. dev.**
Rack rate	$150	100	10	3.16
Corporate rate	$100	175	12	3.46
Discount rate	$75	200	15	3.87
Last minute rate	$30	270	10	3.16
Class	**weighted avg. rate**	**Aggregated mean**	**Aggregated variance**	**Std. dev.**
F1	$150	100	10	3.16
F2	$118	275	22	4.69
F3	$100	475	37	6.08

Linear Programming

Both the threshold method and EMSR method are heuristics, or rules of thumb, that allow businesses to estimate the allocations of capacity to price classes that will maximize revenue. However, more complex methods exist that provide allocations of capacity to rate classes that give the best possible or optimal result. A number of methods are available, and here we discuss how linear programming can be used by a business to maximize its revenue.

The objective of yield management is to maximize the amount of revenue from a fixed resource capacity. The existence of an objective to maximize revenue and known constraints makes linear programming a natural choice in solving this problem.

The basic linear program is shown in Figure 3.6, where the objective is to maximize the revenue (*ri*) from the capacity allocations (*xi*) to each fare class (*i*), subject to two other sets of explicit constraints and one implicit constraint.

The first constraint prevents the capacity being allocated, *xi*, exceeding total capacity, *C*. In our hotel example, the hotel has 500 rooms available to allocate to each of the four fare classes (rack rate, corporate rate, discount rate, and last-minute rate), and the total allocations cannot exceed total capacity of 500. The next set of constraints states that whatever capacity is allocated to each fare class, *xi*, it should not exceed the expected demand, *di*, for that fare class. The last constraint is an implicit constraint that requires both the allocations, *xi*, and the demand, *di*, to be greater than zero, that is, there can be no negative allocations or negative demand.

Using our previous hotel example and assuming that customers only stay for 1 day per visit, the linear program is shown in Figure 3.7, where

$$\max \sum_{i=1}^{n} r_i x_i$$
$$s.t.$$
$$\sum_{i=1}^{n} x_i \leq C$$
$$x_i \leq d_i$$
$$x_i, d_i \geq 0$$

Figure 3.6. Basic linear program

$$
\begin{aligned}
&\max \$150x_1 + \$100x_2 + \$75x_3 + \$30x_4 \\
&s.t. \\
&x_1 + x_2 + x_3 + x_4 \leq 500 \\
&x_1 \leq 100 \\
&x_2 \leq 175 \\
&x_3 \leq 200 \\
&x_4 \leq 270 \\
&x_1, x_2, x_3, x_4 \geq 0
\end{aligned}
$$

Figure 3.7. Linear program for hotel example

rack rate = *x1*; corporate rate = *x2*; discount rate = *x3*; last-minute rate = *x4*.

We can solve this linear program using specialized software or other more generally available software. For example, Microsoft Excel 2007 has a linear programming application using its *Solver* add-in. Using this software, the optimum combination of room rates is provided in Table 3.8.

This solution shows that for the given room rates and assumed levels of demand, the maximum revenue that can be earned for a single night is $48,250. This level of revenue is generated by renting 100 rooms at the rack rate, 175 rooms at the corporate rate, 200 rooms at the discount rate, and 25 rooms at the last-minute rate. Notice that this solution is very similar to the nested EMSR solution provided in Figure 3.5. We would expect this, as nested EMSR is designed to provide a good estimate of the maximum revenue. Also note that all the constraints are binding, except the last-minute rate demand. This means that the

Table 3.8. Linear Programming Example

Objective function	**Final value**			
Maximum revenue	48,250			
Constraints	**Final value**	**Status**	**Slack**	**Shadow price**
Rack rate	100	Binding	0	120.00
Corporate rate	175	Binding	0	70.00
Discount rate	200	Binding	0	45.00
Last minute rate	25	Not binding	245	0.00
Capacity constraint	500	Binding	0	30.00

allocated capacity to these room rates uses all the expected demand and that the solution uses all the hotel capacity. Where the constraint is "not binding," the sum of the allocated value and the slack equals the constraint. For example, for the last-minute rate, the expected demand is 270 = 25 (allocated) + 245 (slack).

For the constraints that are fully used, the solution also provides a *shadow price*. These shadow prices represent the additional revenue that a business could earn if it could relax the constraint by one. For example, if the hotel could increase demand for the rack rate by one, it could increase its revenue by $120, which equals the rack rate of $150 less the $30 of lost revenue from reducing the allocation to the last-minute rate. This reduction is necessary because the hotel room capacity is fully allocated.

These shadow prices can be used as a ranking mechanism, especially where there are numerous products. In our hotel example, we would prioritize relaxing the rack room demand constraint, as it will generate the greatest additional revenue. Ways of relaxing demand constraints include specific marketing to customer groups that increase demand for the product.

In the example provided here, we have focused on a single room type, but for many hotels, there are multiple room types. Further, while some customers may only need a room for a single night, in most cases, customers will stay for multiple, consecutive nights. This "length of stay" problem can also be incorporated into the linear program by adding additional constraints. Each new constraint represents a different room type and length of stay with a corresponding level of demand. Thus, the linear program can reflect the fact that it may be more attractive for a hotel to accept a booking for, for example, five nights at the discount rate rather than for a single night at the rack rate.

Forecasting and Alternative Distributions

Yield management is a large area, and this chapter has only provided simple examples to illustrate how it can be used by businesses. It is important when reviewing this material to appreciate that yield management systems are reliant on the quality of the customer demand forecasts and the appropriateness of the assumptions made. If demand forecasts are not accurate, then the allocations of capacity calculated will not maximize revenue or profits.

Customer demand forecasting is a nontrivial task, given the level of detail required to capture and the ongoing monitoring necessary to ensure forecast accuracy. A variety of methods are available to do this from informal systems that rely on expert judgment (e.g., where the managers use their knowledge of the business to predict sales) to formal econometric forecasting models such as time series models. Forecasting can involve a certain amount of circularity, as demand forecasts for different rate classes are used to set inventory allocations, and these, in turn, can influence the level of customer demand. Reliance on the past to inform future actions always contains the risk that past mistakes will be perpetuated.

For some industries, the data requirements for yield management can be large. For airlines or hotels, for example, reservations are made by the minute and tickets are sold from a variety of distribution outlets, including the Internet, at similar rates. For this reason, in order for protection levels and booking limits to be accurate, demand forecasts and model calculations need to be updated frequently. Further, in this chapter, we have assumed the distributions of demand are known. In the real world, customer demand may not be predictable. Or it may be necessary in particular industries to determine the distribution based on actual data rather than by using theoretical distributions. As with all models, the reliability of any yield management method is dependent on the accuracy of the data and the reliability of the assumptions made.

Summary

This chapter examined how businesses set prices, their relationship with customer demand, and how information about customer demand can be used to maximize revenue. We described different ways that businesses can answer two fundamental questions related to their business:

1. How do I set the prices I charge my customers for the products or services I sell?
2. How much inventory should I allocate to different price levels to maximize my profits?

Answering these questions depends on the nature of the business, its relationship with its customers, the type of customer demand data it can collect, and its ability to link its prices to customers' willingness to pay.

Key Insights

- Strategic pricing (demand-based pricing) links the prices charged to the features that customers value rather than the cost of creating a product or service.
- Yield management uses strategic pricing to maximize revenue by charging customer segments prices that approximate the highest prices they are willing to pay.
- Customers can be segmented by identifying sorting mechanisms that group customers with similar requirements and willingness to pay. The sorting mechanisms used must be capable of keeping customer groups separate so that high-price customers are not converted into low-price customers.
- Various yield management techniques are available to allocate capacity to different customer segments in a way that maximizes revenue. These techniques range from the relatively simple, such as the threshold curve, to the more complex EMSR and linear programming methods.
- All yield management methods need accurate customer demand data to enable predictions to be made about future levels of demand for different groups of customers paying different prices.

CHAPTER 4

Process Management

We haven't got the money so we've got to think.

—Lord Rutherford (Nobel Prize winner; famous for splitting the atom)

You might have the money, but you still have to think hard when it comes to managing processes properly. Processes are where the rubber meets the road, so far as service delivery and making—or not making—money is concerned. These are the activities that the organization performs to provide the service or product that affect revenue streams as well as how resources are consumed. There are three basic concerns with managing processes:

1. The relationships among processes and the order in which the services and products flow
2. The rate or "throughput" at which services and products are provided to customers
3. The variability or fluctuations in activity usage and resource consumption

Throughput determines how much revenue an organization produces. Resource consumption, which is caused by activities such as selling to customers, preparing a meal, or flying an aircraft, is the cost of providing this revenue. We shall see that all of these are interrelated from a revenue management perspective and that efforts for improvement will impact on all three. In this chapter, we will examine these under the following headings:

- Process Mapping
- Throughput and Bottlenecks
- Critical Path Methods for Process Improvement

Process Mapping

A process is the basic building block of both process management and performance measurement. Figure 4.1 describes a process and illustrates that it can contain multiple activities—in this example, there are three. In fact, a process can comprise several processes with each, in turn, comprising a number of activities. Raffish and Turney[1] define *activities* as "work performed within an organization," and "an aggregation of actions performed within an organization that is useful for purposes of activity-based costing." Of course, there can be many processes and activities within any one organization.

Note that processes produce some kind of output and need resources in order to do this. While we often refer to the need to manage costs, the only way that costs can be managed is to manage the underlying processes or activities and their consumption of resources. We shall see in Chapter 5 that simply reducing the consumption of resources does not guarantee that this will reduce costs at all; both consumption and the expenditure on resource capacity must be managed to achieve any cost reductions.

It is also important to understand the relationship among processes and the effect this can have on costs, variability, service quality, and complexity. Figure 4.2 shows three commonly found relationships. Direct relationships refer to processes that are reasonably stand-alone. They have minor relationships with other processes but are fairly autonomous. The

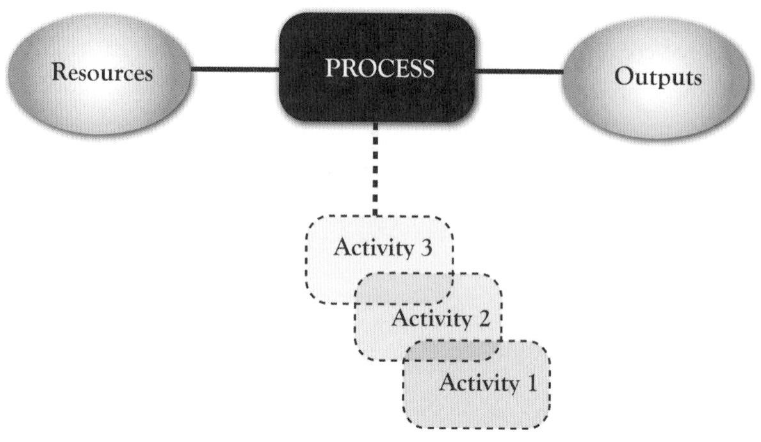

Figure 4.1. Process view with multiple activities

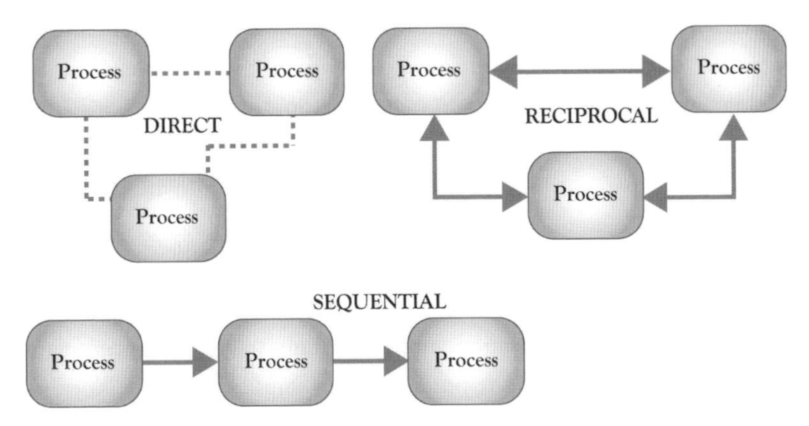

Figure 4.2. Direct, reciprocal, and sequential process relationships

exact opposite applies for reciprocal relationships, where processes are interdependent and interactions occur in no particular order. The third relationship is sequential, where a process is dependent on preceding and successive processes.

Both reciprocal and sequential relationships require a higher level of coordination and potential infrastructure than do direct relationships. There can be greater uncertainty and variability in both sequential and reciprocal relationships, with potentially more in the latter. Given these characteristics, there are generally higher costs, more variability, more problematic service quality, and greater complexity as the process interrelationships move from direct to sequential to reciprocal. In an ideal world, an organization would structure its processes as direct. In reality, this may not be achievable, but efforts should still be made to minimize reciprocal relationships and, where possible, move to sequential and direct relationships. Most service organizations are characterized by sequential relationships and usually the processes and activities are based around employee time. Understanding the sequence and working out what contributes value and what does not is a key feature of revenue management.

Value and Nonvalue-Adding Activities

Overall, organizations are systems of interrelated parts, where the parts are what we are calling processes. The interrelated aspect embodies a key systems theory concept of dynamic behavior among parts that reveals what the organization is about or, in other words, its purpose. Coordinating and managing this requires consideration of how the work is to be allocated in terms of assigning tasks, allocating people and resources to the various parts or processes, and implementing information systems to communicate among these. When functioning well, an organization acts like a reliable machine, doing the jobs when needed. Over time, wear and tear take their toll and bits of the machine begin to function less efficiently. For an organization, nonvalue-adding activities accumulate and breakdowns occur among process relationships. A useful tool for this problem is Porter's value chain (described in Chapter 2), where activities and processes are analyzed to separate out value from nonvalue-adding activities. A simple test is as follows: Examine the outputs provided by each process: do they provide a solution to customer needs or are they needed for the organization to function? For example, bussing the tables in a restaurant is an essential part of customer service; mixing up an order is definitely not. All other activities that do not meet these tests are nonvalue adding and are candidates for elimination or reduction at least. There are what we call "textbook examples" that appear in business textbooks and are fairly obvious. Some examples of these textbook nonvalue-adding activities are shown in Table 4.1.

Adapting some tests from Hansen and Mowen,[2] an activity may be nonvalue added if it meets one of the following conditions:

1. The activity does not produce any change of state, that is, the service or product is not changed by the activity. For example, inspecting is a state-detection activity that does not change the state of the service or product.
2. Preceding activities could have obtained the same change of state. Thus, rework is only necessary because the previous activities were not completed properly. These activities do not have to be internal. For example, what if you could trust your supplier to correctly identify, count, and ship on time? You would not have to check this yourself or waste time sorting out problems with your suppliers.
3. The activity is not essential for other activities to be performed. For example, storing might seem to be required for other activities, but

Table 4.1. Examples of Nonvalue-Adding Activities

Textbook activity	Example 1	Example 2	Example 3
Cost of producing defective products	A restaurant mixing up a dinner order	Software bugs	Misdelivery of mail to wrong address
Machine malfunction or breakdown	Vending machine gives incorrect change	Computer mispricing in a retail store	Breakdowns in equipment at an amusement park
Moving materials or products	Patient movements in a medical center	Maintenance workers making numerous trips to get the right parts and tools	Rearranging materials to get them ready to use
Waiting for work to be completed by a preceding activity	Managing communications for flight delays at airports	Any kind of queue when circumstances are normal	Waiting to receive the bill in a restaurant
Inspecting	Regulatory compliance inspections for minor approvals	Noncritical testing in an audit	Checking that your supplier has delivered the correct materials in the correct quantity at the correct time
Storing	Carrying costs of wine and liquor in a bar	Carrying excessive food ingredients in a restaurant	Old computer files of client jobs that will never be reused

many firms use just-in-time systems, which not only reduce storage requirements but also streamline the materials-supplier interface.

However, it is still not easy to systematically identify nonvalue-adding activities. The following gives some hints on how to do this, but we emphasize that there is no quick solution, and it will involve some serious analysis and thinking:

- Analyze activities: some useful approaches are to use flow charts, service blueprints, or fishbone diagrams. Starting at a high level, chart the major processes in the organization. Then break each process down into smaller processes until you reach the smallest level, which is the activity level.
- Identify value- and nonvalue-adding activities and establish their outputs: this is easier to say than do, although thinking about the outputs of an activity begins to provide some clues as to its value.

> Some helpful hints provided by Baker[3] are summarized in Figure 4.3. There are always "textbook" examples of nonvalue-added activities, as mentioned, such as storing and handling inventories; transporting materials or clients from one part of the firm to another; and redundancies in service configurations. An obvious priority area is to look where clients are waiting for a service to be provided. Remember that this includes internal as well as external clients. The first step is to look for these "textbook" activities and either eliminate or reduce them.

Having examined the "obvious" areas, the second step is to consult with customers about what they do and do not value. Baker sees four outcomes from this step: value-added and nonvalue-added activities, and two transitional outcomes—conditional and zero-based activities. Conditional activities occur either because a service or process is flawed or because we realize that some customers want them. Further analysis (which can include customer profitability analysis) and consultation with customers should assist in deciding into which category they fall. Zero-based activities tend to fall within support or functional areas, such as accounting, marketing, and human resource management. Baker calls them zero based because you should manage them with a zero-based budgeting style, which requires justification for each activity and their resources. The results of a rigorous justification process should assist in deciding what is value adding and nonvalue adding. The first step in this process is to trace resources and costs to activities—this is almost always worth doing in order to get an idea of what an activity costs and what resources it uses. It is also the first stage

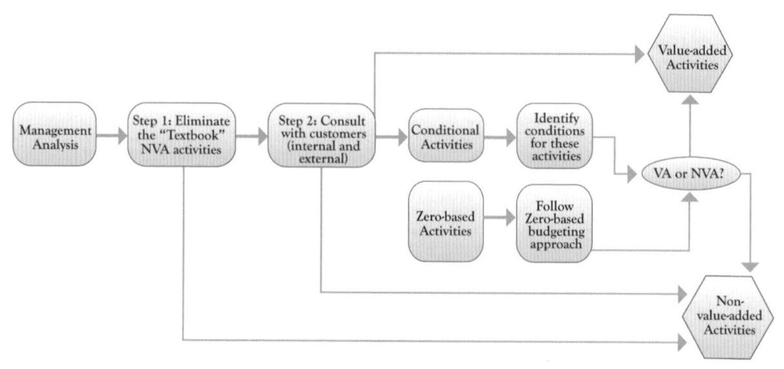

Figure 4.3. Identifying nonvalue-added activities

in developing an activity-based costing system. Knowledge of an activity's cost provides an indication of its materiality and opportunity for cost savings. Tracing resources to activities is not too difficult for most activities and resources, and the more difficult ones can be sidelined for later, more detailed analysis. Bear in mind the adage that it is better to be roughly right than precisely wrong!

The second step is to dig for drivers—this is where the real work comes in, and the previous stages provide some good support for this. We like to think of two types of drivers: cost and revenue. Porter[4] refers to cost drivers as the structural determinants of the cost of an activity, and he points out that they differ in the extent to which an organization controls them. Turney provides further insight: "Cost drivers are factors that determine the work load and effort required to perform an activity. They tell you why an activity is performed and how much effort must be expended to carry out the work."[5] On the other hand, revenue drivers are the determinants of revenue for an activity and are closely related to the firm's strategy, in particular, its marketing and production strategies. To further complicate matters, a cost driver can also be a revenue driver. Consider the rental cost of a retail store. Typical cost drivers are location and occupied space, so it is tempting to think that by shifting location or reducing space, we could save money. But the store might be in a particular location to be near its customers, for example, a fashion boutique in a large shopping mall. Similarly, the marketing strategy might be to provide a sense of spaciousness for the type of customer it is targeting. Identifying key drivers and understanding their roles is crucial in improving process management. Once again, the previous process for identifying value-added activities will call attention to likely revenue drivers.

Third in this process is the benchmarking of activities, where appropriate. Sports teams do it as a matter of course. Organizations talk about it but seldom formalize it. Some managers take it on themselves to watch their competition and understand their processes, always on the outlook for spotting potential waste in their own operations. If you have followed the previous four steps suggested by Baker, you are well positioned for obtaining benefits from benchmarking, particularly combined with the performance analytical methods we will discuss in Chapter 6.

One approach that we will mention here is the half-life measure for continuous improvement, employed at Analog Devices,[6] where the focus in not on the absolute value of the measure but on how fast it is improving. The "half life" denotes how long it takes for a measurement to halve; for example, if customer complaints per month are 100, how many months would it take for them to reduce to 50? The "half" notion is no accident. Analog Devices discovered that when they focused on specific areas (e.g., the percentage of orders shipped late), they found that a small number of causes was responsible for 50% of the problems. They then focused on remedying these causes and, at the end of the cycle, redid the analysis to find the same situation: a small number of causes was responsible for 50% of the problems. The lesson from this is to focus on the priority issues and causes.

There are different names for the various approaches to process management. Management accounting refers to activity-based management; other areas, such as operations management, describe these approaches as value engineering, business process improvement, and process value analysis. The aim of these is the same: analyze activities, find out what drives them, and look for ways to reduce or eliminate nonvalue-adding activities. However, it is not always enough to eliminate or reduce an activity. Chapter 5 will explain that you need to manage both the expenditure on resources and how activities consume these resources. Simply not using a resource will not reduce cost if you are still spending money on it.

When discussing Analog Devices, we mentioned the need to focus on a smaller set of activities and issues. A useful approach is provided in the next section.

Bottlenecks and the Theory of Constraints

Earlier in this chapter, we discussed the interrelatedness of organization activities. Given that even small organizations can be complex, it can be difficult to discern all the relationships among activities. An attempt to improve a particular activity or group of activities can lead to a fall in overall organization performance. Goldratt and Cox[7] emphasize global rather than local solutions; that is, we should focus on the processes from a whole-systems perspective. In order to improve performance and profitability an organization should

- increase throughput; or
- decrease inventory; or

- decrease operating expenses; or
- a combination of the above.

Throughput represents the volume of services or goods sold and is usually measured by revenue minus strictly variable costs (i.e., materials). In a restaurant, throughput would be equal to revenue less food costs. If there are no strictly variable costs, then throughput equals revenue. In the second bullet point, the term "inventory" includes all assets, so this refers more to reducing investment in assets than just concentrating on traditional inventories themselves. The objective is to ensure that the organization does not overinvest in surplus assets. Reducing operating expenses is a familiar objective for all organizations.

In their book *The Goal*, Goldratt and Cox[8] explain this using the main character "Alex Rogo." Alex is asked about recent performance improvements in his factory, and he points to the introduction of robots in the production line, which has greatly improved the efficiencies in processing time in that part of the factory. He is then asked whether this improved throughput (the response is no), did this reduce operating expenses (again, no), or did it reduce inventory (he laughs at this because inventory is going through the roof). His mentor (who goes by the name of Jonah) then tells him that his performance has not improved, as none of these measures has improved. Thus, although local efficiencies improved, the whole system showed no improvement and, in fact, probably worsened.

Goldratt and Cox next introduce the theory of constraints as a focusing mechanism for improving performance. A constraint is anything that limits the organization's ability to perform (for example, to maximize throughput). A restaurant is a good example for illustrating this. Assume that the restaurant is very popular and, at peak periods, has to turn away diners because there is not enough seating. We know that restaurants follow a sequence of activities commencing with the arrival of the customer, ordering and serving a meal, and eventually payment of the bill. According to the theory of constraints, there is always one process or activity that is the bottleneck in this sequence of activities and this bottleneck determines the rate of throughput. There are five steps involved in this analysis:

1. Identify the constraint
2. Exploit the constraint

3. Subordinate everything else to the constraint
4. Elevate the constraint
5. Go back to step one once the constraint is lifted and something else becomes the constraint; do not allow inertia to become a constraint

You should see some similarities to the Analog Devices half-life concept. By repeating these five steps, performance should continue to improve, leading to a process of continuous improvement. Using the restaurant example, we could identify the following five steps:

1. After examining the restaurant operation, we identify insufficient seating as the constraint.
2. Give priority to customers known by the restaurant as regular and good spenders.
3. Improve speed of service and cooking turnaround to improve table turn (i.e., manage meal duration).
4. Investigate whether the restaurant can accommodate more chairs (without overcrowding) by, for example, using outdoor seating or adding a veranda.
5. Doing all the above may shift the constraint so that waiting staff or the kitchen can no longer cope with the number of diners. Back to step one!

Duration management is an interesting concept that not many service organizations always understand or practice well. It refers to managing the length of time or duration that a client spends receiving the service; this is analogous to cycle time in a manufacturing context. Restaurants provide an intuitive example, where the duration starts with the customer being seated and ends when they leave their table; note that it does not necessarily include the time spent waiting for their table[9] or time spent in the bar after their meal. There are some fairly obvious actions that can be taken for managing duration. Menus can be streamlined; waiting staff can avoid suggestive selling of additional menu items, such as dessert or coffee, during busy periods; waiting staff can ensure that the bill is delivered and the payment is processed promptly; and tables can be bussed both during the meal and as soon as the table is vacated. Guests can always be invited to have their coffee or after-dinner drinks in the bar area. Another example is professional accounting services, where peak times tend to be around taxation and reporting deadlines. Suggestive selling of other accounting services would not be beneficial during peak times (of course, obtaining agreement to provide these services off-peak would be beneficial).

In short, such efforts can be made to manage client demands on staff resources in peak times by only offering standardized service, while communicating the availability of lengthier, in-depth service during off-peak times. These are simple examples, and an organization needs to ensure that actions such as increased table turn, extending premises, or streamlining service offerings do not undermine its strategy and positioning.

The strength of Goldratt's approach is that it concentrates on the major issues, namely, those connected with the bottleneck. At some point, the bottleneck can shift to other processes in the service chain. While it is impossible to eliminate all bottlenecks, it is worthwhile to aim toward optimizing the current one. So how do you start with the very first step, identifying the bottleneck? When Alex Rogo asks, "How do you recognize a bottleneck?" Jonah responds, "Look for the machine that has the most inventory waiting to be processed in front of it." It is almost intuitively obvious that the bottleneck is going to be the process that has the biggest queues waiting for it. The five steps focus solely on this bottleneck, which affects the rate of throughput for the whole system. Look at Figure 4.4, which depicts the flow of patients through an outpatient medical facility; using Jonah's guideline, where is the bottleneck?

It is apparent that the largest queue is before the treatment activity, so we would initially conclude that this was the bottleneck. Further analysis would be needed to confirm this, but the key message is that we have now focused on a specific activity for further investigation. Sometimes the bottleneck is not immediately apparent. We know of an elderly woman who was admitted to hospital as the result of a fall in which she injured her leg, leaving her with a nasty wound. The wound was not healing and she was transferred to a ward in another hospital that specialized

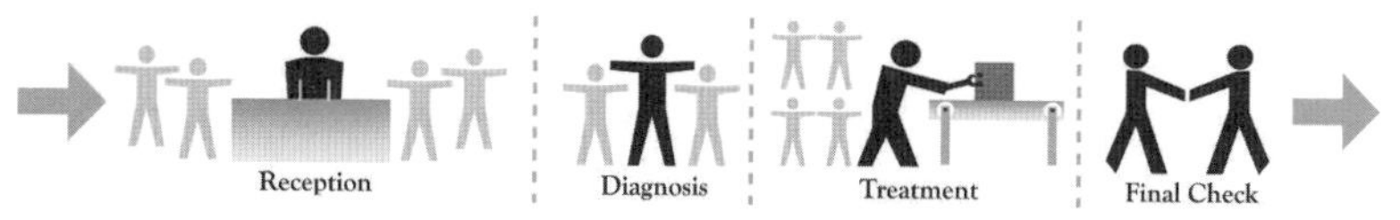

Figure 4.4. Flow of patients through a medical facility

in plastic surgery. The wound treatment was successful and the medical staff had officially discharged her, but the physiotherapist and home-care support staff were concerned about her ability to return home and wanted her transferred to a rehabilitation ward for elderly patients. This is where the bottleneck steps in, because the rehabilitation ward had no spare beds. The result was that the woman remained in a specialist ward (that was in high demand with a waiting list) for an additional 2 weeks, waiting for a bed to become available in the rehabilitation ward. We cannot say for certain whether the rehabilitation or plastic surgery ward was the bottleneck, but we suspect that for elderly patients, the former was the bottleneck.

We now turn to project management that is traditionally associated with projects but that can be easily adapted to process management.

Project Management

Both project and process management are concerned with sequential flows, timing, delays, nonvalue-added activities and bottlenecks (critical paths). To illustrate how project and process management can be used in combination, consider a familiar example: activities in a restaurant. These generally include

- arrival at restaurant and waiting for table;
- seating and order taking;
- cooking;
- serving meals and drinks;
- clearing tables;
- billing.

Assume that we have analyzed a restaurant's activities, and the following information in Table 4.2 is available. The order of the activities is numbered 1 through 25, and the sequence is described by the preceding activities; for example, activities 2 and 3 take place before activity 4. Each activity varies in terms of time, and the range from optimistic to pessimistic, together with the most likely time in minutes, is shown for each. For example, activity 10 can vary between 5 and 15 minutes, with most diners taking around 10 minutes to complete their starters.

Table 4.2. Restaurant Example Showing Activities and Times

Activity	Preceding Activity	Duration (minutes)		
		Optimistic	Most Likely	Pessimistic
1. Host greets	0	1	1	1
2. Wait in bar area if no table	1	0	2	4
3. Seat at table	1, 2	2	2	2
4. Waiter takes bar order	2, 3	3	3	3
5. Bar fills order	4	4	4	10
6. Waiter serves beverage	5	1	1	1
7. Waiter takes menu order	3	5	5	5
8. Kitchen fills starter order	7	5	8	11
9. Waiter serves starter	8	1	1	1
10. Diners finish starter	6, 7, 9	5	10	15
11. Kitchen fills main order	8	10	20	30
12. Bus (clear) table & take beverage order	10	3	3	3
13. Waiter serves main	11	1	1	1
14. Bar fills order	5, 12	4	4	10
15. Waiter serves beverage	14	1	1	1
16. Diners finish main	12, 13, 15	16	20	30
17. Bus table, take dessert, & beverage orders	16	3	3	3
18. Kitchen fills dessert order	11, 17	8	8	8
19. Bar fills order	14, 17	4	4	10
20. Waiter serves beverage	19	1	1	1
21. Waiter serves dessert	18	1	1	1
22. Diners finish dessert	17, 20, 21	12	12	12
23. Bus table and provide bill	22	2	3	10
24. Collect payment	23	2	2	2
25. Customers depart, bus table	24	2	2	2

Figure 4.5 charts these activities, showing the sequences of activities with the bar activities at the top, customer activities in the middle, and kitchen activities at the bottom. There are some key observations from Table 4.2 and Figure 4.5 combined:

1. The activities comprise a network that has starting and end points with intermediate activities.

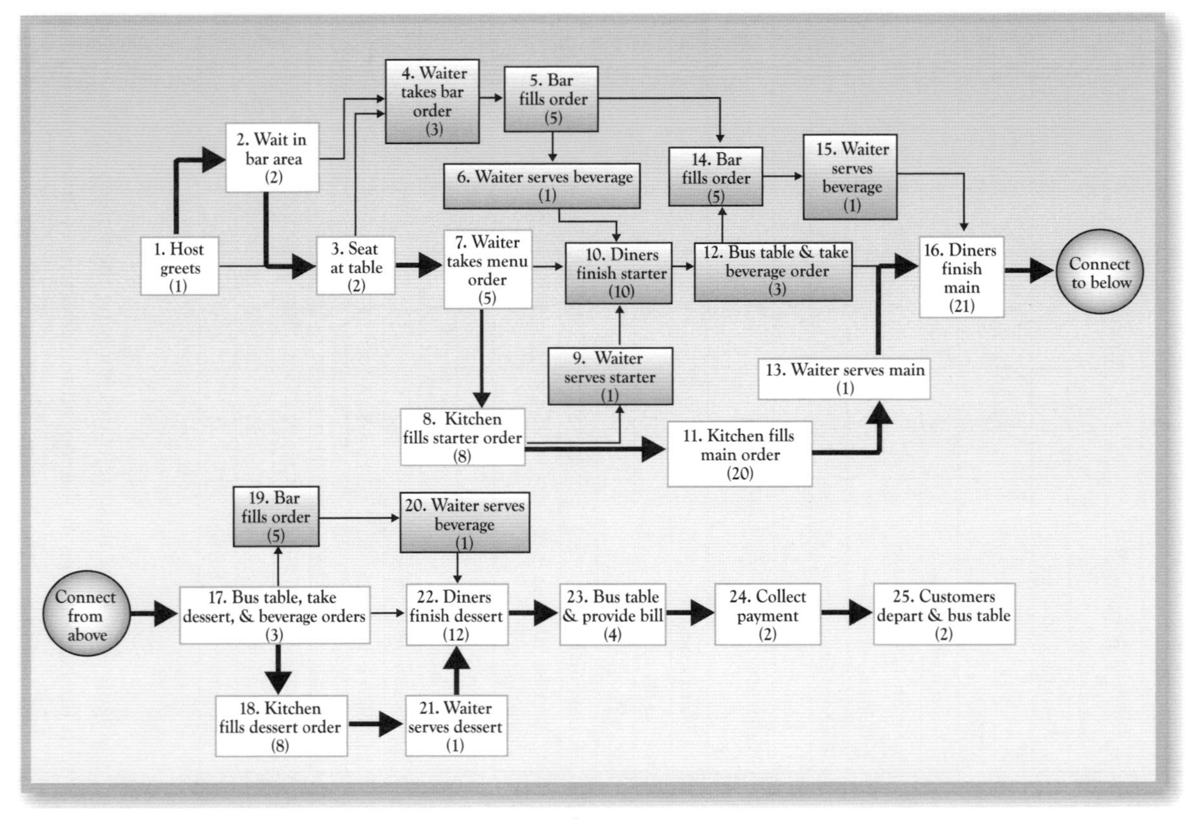

Figure 4.5. Flow of activities in restaurant example

2. Some activities run parallel to others, for example, the bar, customer, and kitchen.
3. Some activities must obviously be completed before others, for example, 4 and 5 must be completed before 6.
4. There is variability in the time among activities (e.g., compare the times between activities 3 and 7) as well as within an activity (e.g., in activity 16, diners can take between 16 to 30 minutes to finish their main course).

We are going to use this information to identify the critical path showing the longest time for a customer to dine in this restaurant. The critical path is the longest chain (in time) of dependent activities within the network, which, in a project context, is how long it takes to complete the project. We shall also show how to identify areas where this process can be improved.

Where does the number come from?

We calculate the expected time for each activity using the optimistic, most likely, and pessimistic estimates. We want to give more weight to the most likely times so we use the following formula:

$$\text{expected activity time} = \frac{o + 4m + p}{6}$$

where optimistic, most likely, and pessimistic are represented by o, m, and p, respectively, and most likely is weighted by four. For example we would calculate the expected time for activity 16 (diners finish main) as:

$$\text{expected activity time} = \frac{16 + 4 \times 20 + 30}{6} = \frac{126}{6} = 21$$

In our restaurant example, the critical path identifies the activities that determine how long it takes from the time the customer is greeted to the time the customer leaves. Figure 4.5 shows that there are some paths that are parallel to others, and if you count the times on those paths, you will find that one path will be longer than the other. For example, activities 4, 5, and 6 take 3, 4, and 1 minutes, respectively, which totals 8 minutes.

The parallel stream of activities 7 and 8 take 5 and 8 minutes, respectively, which totals 13 minutes. It will therefore take longer to take the menu order and fill the starter than to take the drinks order and fill those. In Figure 4.5, the critical path is shown by the large arrows and nonshaded activities. Notice that we did not include activity 9 in our comparison because it does not affect the time taken in total to service the customer, as while the starter is being served, the kitchen is preparing the main course. Adding up the times for the activities on the critical path, we get 92 minutes.

Where Does the Number Come From?

Activities: 1 2 3 7 8 11 13 16 17 18 21 22 23 24 25;

Times for each: 1+ 2+ 2+ 5+ 8+ 20+ 1+ 21+ 3+ 8+ 1+ 12+ 4+ 2+ 2 = 92 minutes.

This means that customers will spend, on average, 92 minutes in the restaurant. We can also work out that they will spend 30 minutes waiting.

Where does the number come from?

2 minutes in the bar waiting for a table, 9 minutes waiting for the starter, 10 minutes for the main, and 9 minutes for dessert.

While customers may be quite happy to wait and look at the view or enjoy the ambience, there is a point at which waiting becomes not just nonvalue adding but value detracting. We might like to know the likelihood of a customer spending over 100 minutes in the restaurant, and this can be determined using the information about optimistic and pessimistic times, as shown in the sidebar. There is a 5% chance that a customer will spend longer than 100 minutes; in the opposite perspective, we can say there is a 5% chance that a customer will spend less than 84 minutes in the restaurant. We can estimate the likelihood of the times anywhere along the critical path. For example, we can say that, on average, it will take 39 minutes from entering the restaurant for a customer to receive their main course and that the likelihood of this taking longer than 50 minutes is less than 1%. It is, however, important to bear in mind that this still represents one customer or table for every 100.

Where does the number come from?

In addition to the expected time, we need a measure of the variability for each activity. One common way of calculating this is using the following formula illustrating with activity 16:

$$\text{var} = \left(\frac{p - o}{6}\right) = \left(\frac{30 - 16}{6}\right) = 5.4$$

Calculating this for each activity on the critical path and summing gives a total of 23.3 for the total variance. The standard deviation (4.8) is the square root of this total and using a Normal distribution we can calculate the probability of the time exceeding 100 minutes.

So how could a restaurant use this information? Knowledge of the critical path and variability of the activities on it provides opportunities for exploring ways to shorten it. Some possibilities include speeding up some of the activities, such as greeting, order taking, serving, bussing, and billing; preparing food ahead of time; changing the menu to items that require less preparation time; and beginning to prepare the main course before completion of the starter order. If the critical path is shortened, capacity increases (or is used more efficiently), as more customers are then served within the available opening hours. This increases revenue and profitability, although there may be additional costs involved, such as the hiring and training of staff. Reducing waiting time may also increase customer satisfaction and demand.

But there can be a downside! Reducing portion sizes and speeding up the process (e.g., taking orders earlier, changing menu choices) may reduce demand, revenue, and profitability. An organization needs to think strategically and consider what customers want before reducing service cycle time. Otherwise, there is the risk of failing to meet customer expectations as well as putting too much stress on staff so that service deteriorates. However, there may be periods when being able to guarantee the dining time is a key advantage, such as when customers are going to see a show following their meal.

Summary

Process management is the nonvisible side of revenue management. While pricing and yield management tend to be external and obvious to customers and competitors, processes, by their very nature, are internal and less visible. However, they become very visible when they fail and service delivery or production is affected. In this chapter, we have provided some tools to analyze processes in order to identify their relationships with each other and with the overall organization structure. Focusing on value- and nonvalue-adding evaluations keeps the revenue management goal prominent. But global, as opposed to local, improvements are the goal. A useful focusing tool is to identify the bottleneck and follow Goldratt's five focusing steps. Closely related is the use of project management to manage the process. Project management has well-developed approaches and methods, but it is an overlooked tool for organizations to better manage their processes.

Key Insights

- Organization design is a major cost driver; pay attention to process relationships and reduce variability within a process as much as possible.
- Start with the "textbook" examples of nonvalue-added activities (NVA) and then consult your customers to identify your specific NVA.
- The bottleneck sets the rate of throughput (i.e., revenue and expenses) and is the primary focus of improving processes and revenue.
- Project manage the process! You will understand the flows better, and there are well-established project management tools that provide insights for improving resource usage.

CHAPTER 5

Cost and Capacity Management

I've never seen a cost walking around, have you?

—Anonymous

Introduction

Given the close relationship between revenue and cost, you will waste the effort that you devote to revenue management if you do not pay close attention to managing cost. Most often, what drives revenue also drives cost; an increase in revenue causes an increase in cost. But how much cost? There are many ways of measuring cost, and its size depends on the way you measure it—whether as full cost, variable cost, direct cost, or activity-based cost, to mention a few—and variations on each of these. However elusive cost may seem, we know it when it hits. As mentioned in Chapter 4, we cannot manage costs, only activities. You carry out activities to conduct your business, the activities consume resources, and the costs arrive.

You may be aware of a number of ways of treating costs, each of which has its uses, such as activity-based costing, cost-volume-profit analysis, life-cycle costing, and target costing. We (the authors) favor activity-based costing (ABC) because it connects so strongly to activities. An organization's activities consume resources, and provided you design a good ABC system, it allows you to track those costs and to follow them through to outputs. When we get to put dollar values to resources, activities, and outputs, the strong connection between activities and ABC gives more realistic numbers than other ways of doing this. ABC is particularly revealing when the organization has (a) a high proportion of overheads in its cost structure, and (b) considerable diversity in its activities or outputs, which means that resource consumption patterns differ across activities and outputs. Organizations delivering services generally meet the first condition because they can trace few of their resources to their outputs. For example, restaurants can usually trace little more than the cost of food to a meal served in a restaurant. Many service-delivery organizations also meet the second condition.

Remember, at this point, that the dollar cost of resources consumed is not equal to the cash outlay on resources. ABC shows you the amount of resources consumed irrespective of whether you have paid for them, and irrespective of whether you have brought in those resources for immediate consumption or whether they represent a share of depreciation (i.e., part of the cost of a building or equipment used).

In the first part of this chapter, we describe and examine the use of ABC systems in service-delivery organizations. In the rest of the chapter, we focus on a cost driver that is of considerable importance to most service-delivery organizations—capacity.

Resource Consumption

Figure 4.1 illustrated a simple service-delivery process made up of various activities. It also provides a basis for both managing and assigning costs. It is important that those responsible for designing cost systems understand how the business operates in terms of the ways in which services are created and delivered. In order to model the cost of any process, you must first understand the process, what it produces, and how its activities consume resources.

Figure 5.1 represents the resource consumption process. To visualize this, think about the sequence followed in starting a new business. You would start with what the business is trying to achieve and its planned outputs. The next step would be to design the processes and activities needed to provide these outputs. The activities would need different types of resources. For example, once you have decided the types of activities in a service center, this will lead to the required skills and number of workers. Thus, how you select and resource the activities to provide the outputs will determine the cost drivers that underlie the activities.

Figure 5.1. Resource consumption

Cost Drivers

The Consortium for Advanced Manufacturing-International identifies cost drivers as the root causes of costs,[1] and, in the same vein, Turney[2] recommends that managers should "dig for drivers." Once managers have identified the major cost drivers in a business, they can take steps to modify or eliminate them in order to improve the firm's cost structure. On the other hand, care must be taken that actions to improve cost management do not adversely affect the organization's revenues.

Figure 5.2 shows revenue drivers and cost drivers. It recognizes that a cost driver may simultaneously be a revenue driver. Chapter 4 described the location of a retail store as both a revenue and cost driver. Similarly, a major cost driver for a university may be its research culture. However, the research reputation of the university may also be a major revenue driver because it attracts students to its undergraduate and postgraduate courses.

Shank and Govindarajan distinguish between structural and executional cost drivers.[3] An organization makes decisions about its economic structure, including issues such as scale, scope, experience, technology,

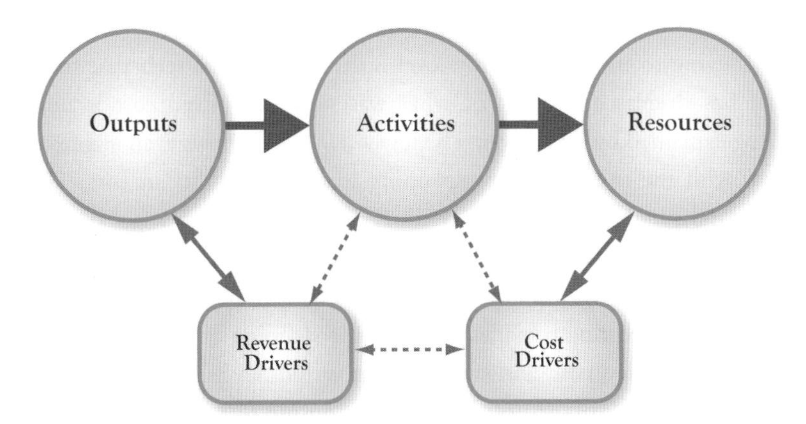

Figure 5.2. Revenue drivers, cost drivers, and resource consumption

and complexity. These decisions shape the organization's structural cost drivers. Executional cost drivers include work-force involvement, total quality management, capacity utilization, plant layout, product configuration, and linkages with suppliers and customers. These drivers relate to a firm's ability to "execute" (carry out operations) effectively. In the short term, these cost drivers cannot usually be modified significantly; thus, their associated costs are difficult to change—they tend to be regarded as "committed costs." For example, it is difficult to change scale, scope, location, or product configuration in the short term. Since activity-based systems are designed to facilitate strategic decisions, it is best to take a long-term view of cost behavior when working with these systems.

In the longer term, identifying and understanding cost drivers provide opportunities not just to change structures and processes but also to reevaluate strategy and policy. The ability to relax or reduce the effects of cost drivers by changing strategy can determine how successful an organization is in its efforts toward continuous improvement.

Hierarchy of Activities

Figure 5.3 shows four graphs of cost behavior corresponding to four levels of activity. The vertical axis shows total cost and the horizontal axis shows a driver volume. Level 1 total cost is split into variable and fixed costs. The variable cost is explained by the level 1 driver, but there is a large amount of fixed costs that is left unexplained. This is similar to traditional cost-volume profit analysis. We therefore introduce further levels and drivers to try to dig into the unexplained fixed cost.

Moving to the graph of the level 2 driver, it can be seen that fixed cost has decreased, as part of what was previously fixed cost is now being explained by this driver. The lower left graph shows even less fixed cost, with the level 3 driver explaining further variability in cost. The lower right-hand graph reveals residual fixed cost because selected drivers explain further cost behavior. Looking at the reduction in fixed costs between the top left graph and the lower right graph, we can see how activity-based costing provides greater understanding of the relationship between activities, cost, and the drivers at various levels. We can arrange the different types of drivers and their relationship to activity cost behavior in the form of a hierarchy.

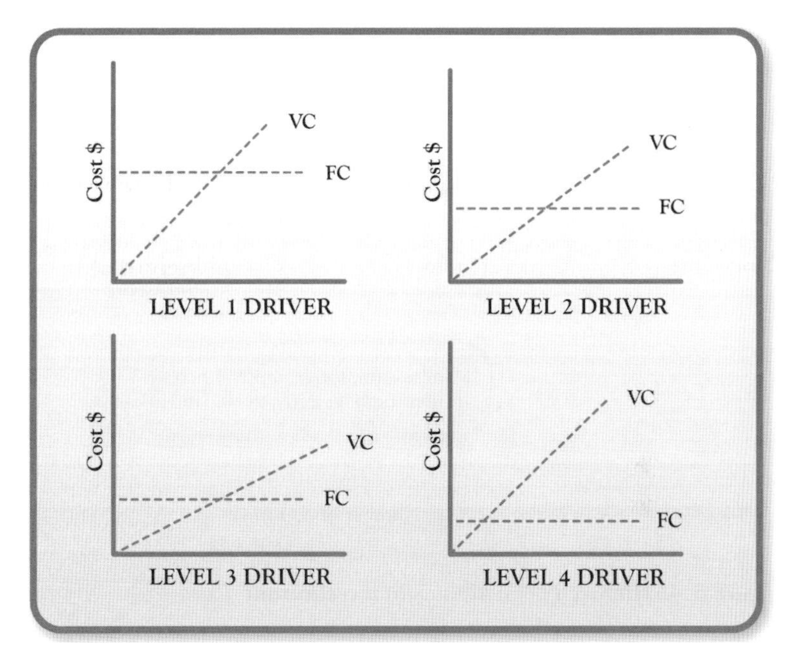

Figure 5.3. Cost behavior at different activity levels

Based on manufacturing activities, Cooper and Kaplan[4] suggest a hierarchy that reflects different resource consumption patterns at each level. This hierarchy is unit level, batch level, product sustaining, and facility (organization) sustaining. By identifying the relevant hierarchy, or hierarchies, of activities for an organization, we gain another powerful insight into resource consumption patterns. For example, product-sustaining resource consumption can be as significant, if not more so, than unit-level consumption for some organizations. Although hierarchies are likely to be similar in nature to the basic format (unit level, batch level, product sustaining, and facility [organization] sustaining), we can develop hierarchies that suit the characteristics of the organization and its activities. Figure 5.4[5] illustrates how the hierarchy could be applied to a restaurant.

Starting at the unit level, you can identify resources that directly vary with the number of customers, such as food ingredients, drinks, or napkins. Other costs vary more with the meal sessions and are only indirectly related to the number of customers (batch level); for example, a different number of staff may be scheduled for lunch as opposed to dinner.

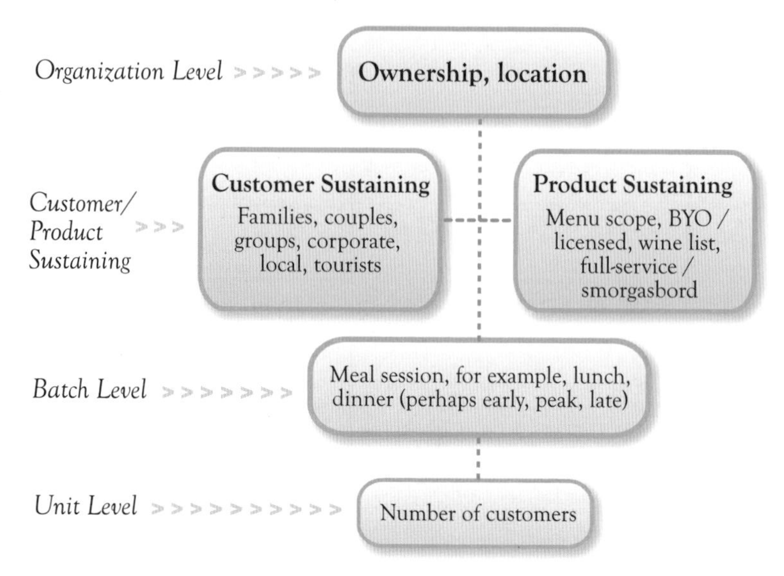

Figure 5.4. Hierarchy of activities in a restaurant

Source: Maguire and Rouse (2004).

Some activities and related costs can vary according to customer type; for example, some restaurants cater to children whereas others may focus on corporate or large groups. These costs are customer sustaining. At a similar level, product sustaining includes activities and costs associated with creating and maintaining the product or service, such as the scope of a restaurant's menu, full service versus smorgasbord, licensed or unlicensed. The final level captures the remaining infrastructural activities and costs, such as rent, senior management, and taxes.

The hierarchy provides valuable insights into potential courses of action for improving the management of resources, capacity, and throughput. Even if the costs identified are only approximate for each level, this knowledge enables you to investigate strategic alternatives. It also provides a general description of how the activities of the organization map onto its strategy

Most people work with the idea that costs vary with volume (i.e., the number of units). The hierarchy shows that resource consumption patterns differ across levels in the hierarchy. For example, to a large extent, the cost of food ingredients varies with the number of customers. Customer volume does not explain many other costs. If we move up a level to batch-level costs, we could expect resource consumption to vary with the number of dining sessions. While restaurants attempt to have the appropriate number of staff to meet expected demand in each dining session, this is not always successful. Staffing costs are more likely to be driven by the number of dining sessions (e.g., lunch and dinner).

There are a number of strategic decisions that a restaurant makes; this involves issues such as the scope of its menu (a buffet option or a la carte only), or the availability of alcohol (licensed premises or bring your own [BYO]). These choices drive costs at the product-sustaining level; for example, licensed premises may require a different restroom configuration, call for a wine inventory and associated carrying costs, as well as additional management activities. At the customer-sustaining level, the cost of these activities can vary depending on the customer type. We explore this later in this chapter when we discuss customer profitability analysis.

The hierarchy provides a simple and effective method for understanding a service organization's cost structure in terms of strategic choices and different levels of cost behavior. Moving to more effective cost management requires that we dig for the underlying cost drivers. We have seen that these cost drivers often strongly relate to the way in which organizations derive revenue. As mentioned earlier in this chapter, capacity represents a significant resource and capacity utilization is a major cost driver. We devote much of the rest of the chapter to this topic.

Capabilities and Capacity Management

While some use the terms "capacity" and "capability" interchangeably, and there does not appear to be a formal distinction between them, their meanings are not identical. The dictionary definitions refer to capability in terms of ability or use for a specific purpose, and capacity in terms of the ability to receive, hold, or absorb a volume. Strategy influences both capabilities and capacity, and it takes time to establish both.

The resource-based view (RBV) has developed to explain how organizations achieve competitive advantage. From this perspective, organizations focus internally, much as we did when we examined core competencies in Chapter 2. There is a close connection between capabilities and core competencies, and the distinction between them is not immediately clear. Stalk[6] suggests that "capabilities are the mechanisms by which core competencies are made into realities." This links to our discussion in Chapter 2, which illustrated the close connection between capabilities and core competencies.

The RBV uses industry structure as a basis for understanding strategy. Competitive advantage essentially relies on monopoly power by finding a gap amid the bargaining powers and threats in the industry. This power may be ephemeral in that other organizations may be able to imitate the actions of those that hold the competitive advantage. The RBV suggests that organizations focus on their resources, which may hold the key to competitive advantage. But if all industry players are able to obtain these resources, it would not be enough to focus on resources; capabilities provide competitive advantage because they are inimitable. Wal-Mart's challenge to K-Mart rode, to some extent, on its revision of the "entire value delivery system."[7] This capability stretches across the value chain presented in Chapter 2. But competitive advantage demands more—dynamic capabilities, which derive from the ability to integrate, build, and reconfigure internal and external competences to address rapidly changing environments.[8] The activities comprising capabilities such as service delivery and marketing are clearly central to both cost management and revenue management. Figure 5.5 depicts dynamic capabilities, capabilities, competencies, and capacity and shows how they relate to the value chain.

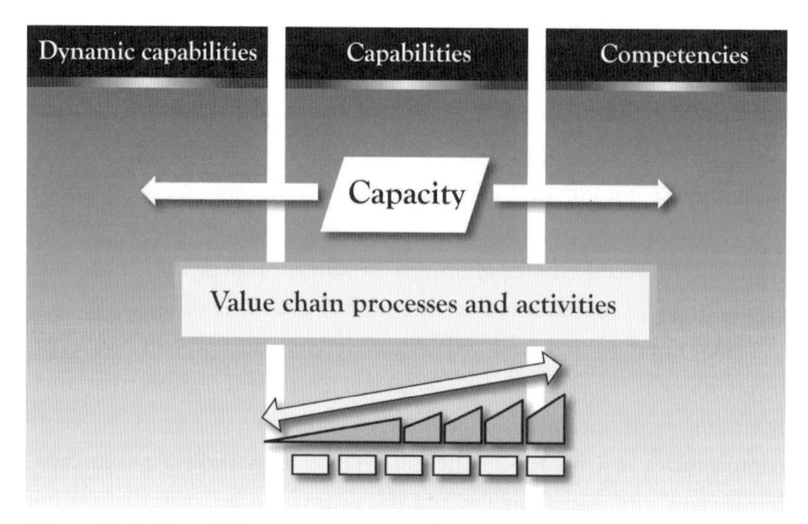

Figure 5.5. Capabilities, capacity, and the value chain

Although capacity is one of many cost drivers, its management may be critical for the performance of your organization, and the way in which you assign capacity cost potentially has a significant effect on capacity management. Capacity management is central to service-delivery organizations, as is apparent from Figure 1.1 in Chapter 1. While a manufacturing organization is able to produce for inventory when capacity exceeds demand, service-delivery organizations cannot do this. Empty bed-nights in a hotel, empty seats on an aircraft, and empty seats in a restaurant represent potential revenue lost. Available capacity is thus a serious constraint on managers' freedom of action in a service-delivery organization. Notwithstanding this, managers can take actions to moderate the impact of capacity on performance by making appropriate arrangements with suppliers (speed of delivery), employees (working hours), and new and existing customers (delivery patterns and service levels).

Both the planning and management of resource acquisition and operations in a perfect world would be so accurate that available capacity and resource usage match exactly. In practice, we may overestimate requirements or resources may be "lumpy" (e.g., we may be able to acquire resources only in specified quantities). For example, we may acquire factory space that exceeds the space required by activities, thus leaving space unused. Further, the resources supplied to a particular activity may exceed the resources demanded by the outputs.

At both points, there is unused capacity, representing the difference between resources acquired and resources consumed. This has potential implications for the cost of outputs, which we consider later in this chapter.

Acquiring and Consuming Resources

Some resources are used immediately and this is assured where a business applies just-in-time principles; materials are used immediately, as are short-term labor and purchased services. Where resources are not used immediately, such as premises under long-term lease, or workers under long-term contract, they provide capacity for activities over a period of time.

Maguire and Heath draw a distinction between capacity management and capacity costing, such that capacity management is a broad concept of which capacity costing is a subset, as capacity management concerns decisions about the optimal use of existing facilities and also decisions about expansion, contraction, replacement, or the use of alternative technologies.

For costing purposes, capacity is defined and measured in terms of the facility being used to provide the product or service. The theoretical capacity of a facility is therefore defined in terms of that facility. It excludes speculation about future technologies or even whether the facility is the most appropriate facility given the task being performed.[9]

What Is the Capacity of Your Business?

How would you go about measuring capacity? A variety of definitions of capacity exist; in general, the capacity constraint represents the committed resources in the business that managers are responsible for making the best use of, and unused capacity represents wasted resources. To manage capacity, we need to define what is meant by available capacity and then measure capacity utilization. The following are some commonly used capacity measures:[10]

- Theoretical capacity represents the maximum output that a plant or process can produce given the existing facilities, assuming that there is no down time, even for preventative maintenance. For example, the level of output if a plant operated 24 hours a day, 7 days a week, 365 days a year. (But note the definition of theoretical capacity in the next section.)
- Practical capacity represents the capacity level attainable by a process or plant where no special steps are taken to extend the level of output. It is calculated by adjusting theoretical capacity for normal downtime (e.g., setups, preventative maintenance, and workers' rest periods).
- Normal capacity represents the expected or average capacity utilized over a number of periods (for example, the average utilization over 5 prior years). Using normal capacity smoothes the impact of fluctuating utilization levels that can result from using an estimate based on a single prior year.
- Budgeted capacity is the budgeted utilization for the next period.

- Actual capacity utilization is the ex post facto of capacity utilized during the period.

Figure 5.6 shows the relationship among the capacity measures most commonly used.

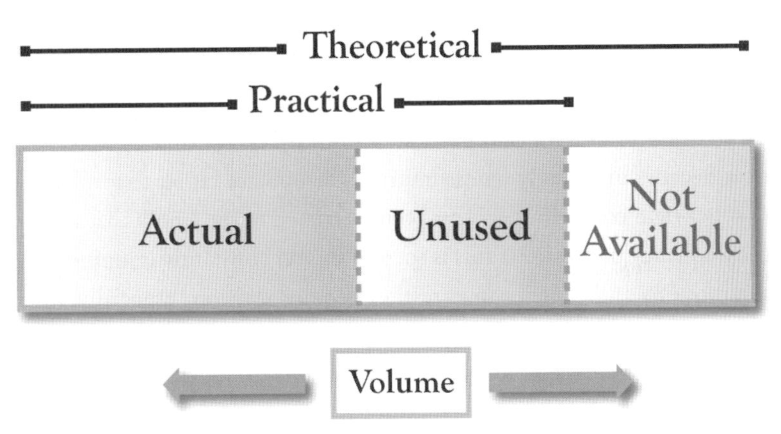

Figure 5.6. Capacity concepts

Theoretical Capacity

The theoretical capacity of a facility is the maximum sustainable rate of output over its estimated useful life.[11] A "sustainable" rate implies a level of output that persists for a considerable period of time. Further, a facility usually ages over its useful life, with a decline in its productivity, which results in a decline in theoretical capacity. In theory, businesses could operate continuously, 24 hours a day, 7 days a week (24/7). However, in practice, there are only a few businesses, such as restaurants and bars, that operate in this way—most organizations do not, and, accordingly, it is not appropriate to specify theoretical capacity in terms of 24/7. Depending on demand conditions, most manufacturers work only one shift (8 hours) or two shifts (16 hours) a day, rather than three shifts (24 hours), even if they have the option to produce for inventory. Similarly, most service organizations do not operate 24/7. Restaurants face no demand at three o'clock in the morning, and bus operators have few, if any, customers between midnight and, say, five o'clock in the morning.

Practical Capacity

As shown in Figure 5.6, not all theoretical capacity is available for use due to scheduled maintenance, machine setups, workers' holidays, and lunch or other breaks. Practical capacity measures the capacity level available from a process or plant without taking special steps to extend it. It represents theoretical capacity minus capacity that is not available for use.

In service organizations, there is often limited plant or equipment, and available people hours represent most, or all, of a service provider's capacity. In this case, a significant portion of so-called unavailable capacity may exist because of underlying assumptions or policies rather than physical or other rigid constraints such as policies related to the length of a shift or the frequency of breaks. If this is so, you should constantly examine these assumptions and policies in case they require revision, especially when circumstances change. Failure to do this can build in waste.[12]

You have a choice as to the treatment of the nonoperating hours that are determined by demand conditions. You could specify theoretical capacity in terms of a 24/7 operation and treat the nonoperating hours as unavailable capacity, or you could regard those hours as outside the definition of theoretical capacity. The second option makes sense, as it excludes hours from theoretical capacity when there is no realistic expectation of demand. This option also allows managers to monitor unavailable capacity that arises due to prevailing policies and assumptions, thus facilitating capacity management.

Of all the capacity definitions, only practical capacity allows us to distinguish between used and unused capacity. Gantt[13] was the first to advocate the use of practical capacity as a volume base for product costing, because (a) it maintains a stable cost per unit irrespective of fluctuations in volume, and (b) volume fluctuations do not affect performance measurement.

A simple example brings out the first point. Nutrilearn supplies nutritious but inexpensive lunches to some 25 schools. The variable cost per lunch is $3 and its annual fixed costs of capacity are $7.3 million. Table 5.1 shows the budgeted figures for 2010 and 2011, and the practical capacity in terms of the number of lunches.

We want to calculate the budgeted capacity cost and the practical capacity cost per lunch. If management bases its prices on cost, the unit

Table 5.1. Nutrilearn: Budgets and Practical Capacity

	in thousands
Budgeted capacity lunches for 2010	2,555
Budgeted capacity lunches for 2011	2,150
Practical capacity (lunches)	3,650
Annual fixed costs of capacity (committed costs)	$7,300

cost will have an important influence on price. Although Nutrilearn might not have many competitors providing school lunches, there are many catering businesses that could enter the market, which means that pricing is an important issue.

We note from Table 5.1 that Nutrilearn has budgeted 405,000 fewer lunches (2,555,000–2,150,000) for 2011 than it did for 2010. Table 5.2 shows the effect on the total cost per unit using budgeted capacity volumes for each year. If it bases its prices on costs, Nutrilearn could be tempted to increase their price to compensate on the basis of the increased cost per unit ($6.40 versus $5.86; see Table 5.2). The reduction in business may be the result of decreased demand. For example, economic conditions could be causing fewer schools to sign up, competitors could be increasing their share of the market, or new competitors could have entered the market. Whatever the cause, a price increase could reinforce these influences, which would reduce the level of business further, leading to further price increases. This cycle of decline is frequently referred to as the "death spiral."

Table 5.2 shows the cost of practical capacity per lunch ($2), derived by dividing the total cost of practical capacity ($7,300,000) by the number of lunches (3,650,000) that Nutrilearn is able to provide with that capacity. This means that the cost of practical capacity per lunch remains the same irrespective of changes in budgeted or actual output levels. If

Table 5.2. Nutrilearn: Capacity Cost and Total Cost Per Lunch

Capacity allocation base	**Annual Fixed Costs (in thousands of dollars)**	**Number of lunches (in thousands)**	**Annual Fixed Costs per lunch**	**Variable cost per lunch**	**Total cost per lunch**
Budgeted capacity 2010	$7,300	2,555	$ 2.86	$ 3.00	$ 5.86
Budgeted capacity 2011	$7,300	2,150	$ 3.40	$ 3.00	$ 6.40
Practical capacity	$7,300	3,650	$ 2.00	$ 3.00	$ 5.00

Nutrilearn uses this cost as its basis for pricing, it avoids the death spiral. Note that if managers refer to the market to set prices, fluctuations in cost do not affect them (see Chapter 3).

Performance and Capacity Usage Reports

Gantt's[14] second point is that if practical capacity is used, volume fluctuations do not affect performance measurement and can also be useful to highlight the extent of unused capacity and its cost. Table 5.3 illustrates the effect of using practical capacity to report used and unused capacity as budgeted for 2010 and 2011, in terms of both number of lunches and dollars.

When unused capacity is separately identified, we are able to take appropriate action, such as increasing throughput to utilize the unused capacity or reducing the level (and cost) of available capacity. However, when we decide on the appropriate action, we need to consider that increasing throughput could reduce the spare capacity we have available to provide superior service to customers,[15] and that if we reduce capacity, it can be difficult to increase it again. In particular, if key employees with specialized skills are made redundant, it may be difficult or costly to replace them. The same applies to special equipment. Accordingly, it may be better to carry the cost of some unused capacity unless we are certain that demand will not increase again in the future.

By identifying and analyzing activities and applying ABC, we are able to ascertain the practical, used, and unused capacity for each activity. We can then incorporate this information in performance reports and enhance capacity management, as shown in the next example.[16]

An important distinction for capacity costing is between resources that are used when supplied and those that are committed. Consider an

Table 5.3. Nutrilearn: Used and Unused Capacity

Lunches	**Practical capacity in thousands**	**Used in thousands**	**Unused in thousands**
Budgeted 2010	3,650	2,555	1,095
Budgeted 2011	3,650	2,150	1,500
Dollars			
Budgeted 2010	$7,300	5,110	2,190
Budgeted 2011	$7,300	4,300	3,000

example of an organization, Downtown Caterers, which operates in a metropolitan area, providing catering services. It employs mainly short-term labor to prepare food and serve at catering functions. Managers and chefs are appointed on long-term contracts and are, therefore, treated as committed costs. Committed costs are those costs that are ongoing and cannot be reduced or eliminated, at least in the short run. Raw food and short-term labor are clearly not capacity costs, as you can avoid them if they are not required.

The report in Table 5.4 shows the cost of unused capacity of the committed resources for three activities: preparation, marketing, and customer service. This report allows managers to focus on performance areas related to the use of resources. For example, the preparation activity has one quarter of its total cost attributed to unused capacity. In the absence of this information, top management may hold the activity manager responsible for an increase in the unit cost of the service, when the real reason for the increase could be a decline in the number of functions.

In most organizations, capacity reporting for every activity is likely to cause information overload. To avoid this, management should apply the 80-20 rule, where 20% of the activities account for 80% of the cost

Table 5.4. Downtown Caterers performance report

Performance report for May 2010	Used (in thousands of dollars)	Unused (in thousands of dollars)	Total (in thousands of dollars)
Revenue			150
Resources supplied as used			
Raw food	20		
Short-term labor	45		65
Contribution			85
Committed resources			
Preparation	30	10	
Marketing	10	2	
Customer service	10	3	
Total of committed resources	50	15	
Cost of capacity used			50
Profit on capacity used			35
Cost of unused capacity			15
Operating profit			20

of capacity. Managers will then be able to monitor and manage capacity utilization of only the most significant activities.

Theory of Constraints

It may seem that this activity-based approach to managing capacity is in conflict with the theory-of-constraints (TOC) approach referred to in Chapter 4. According to the TOC, we should ignore unused capacity in the nonconstrained activities. This is contrary to the activity-based capacity management approach outlined here, where we identify unused capacity in all major activities, with a view to taking action. While some authors have attempted to reconcile the two approaches, we are not convinced that it has been fully achieved. One suggestion is that activity-based capacity management is oriented toward the long term, while TOC focuses on the short term. We suggest calculating used and unused capacity for major nonconstrained activities, so that it both informs the strategic orientations and makes this information available when the bottleneck shifts. We then apply the five TOC steps (outlined in Chapter 4) while noting the strategic implications.

Optimal Capacity

As indicated, we can extract useful information for capacity management by identifying and measuring practical capacity. No matter how much care we take in specifying practical capacity, it does not necessarily represent an optimum. While optimal capacity may not be easy to quantify, it is useful to conceptualize this point because it may spur further improvement.[17] Not all unused capacity is waste. For a business following a differentiation strategy, unused capacity may add value by allowing it to provide superior service to customers.[18] For a business of this type, there is an opportunity cost attached to the unused capacity as capacity utilization approaches relatively high levels. Capacity utilization is optimal where marginal contribution is equal to the marginal cost of capacity-related costs. Provided marginal contribution exceeds the marginal cost of capacity-related costs, it is worthwhile to increase output to the practical capacity level. In this case, the output level at optimal capacity utilization is the same as that at practical capacity. If there are changes in the marginal contribution or the marginal cost, they may reach equality (indicating optimal capacity utilization) before the practical capacity level is reached. Additional capacity-related costs can dramatically increase as utilization approaches practical capacity. For example, if an organization becomes less flexible in responding to customer requests, it may not be able to charge a superior price based on a differentiation strategy that relies on flexibility. It may therefore have to lower prices, which lowers its marginal contribution. Or its marginal cost may increase due to congestion, as resources become stretched and the organization is forced to incur overtime costs or suffers higher costs due to errors made when people work under pressure. Thus, the optimal level of capacity can occur before practical capacity is reached.

Fluctuating Demand

Many businesses face fluctuating demand due to, for example, different seasons of the year, holiday periods, or times of the day. Ski resorts and beach resorts are often busy only during particular seasons and are quiet the rest of the year. Similarly, some businesses are much busier at some times of the day or week than others (for example, bus services, movie theaters, and restaurants). Some businesses can be subject to both influences; for example, airlines can be influenced both by times of the day for commuter services and by seasons of the year for services to tourist destinations. If businesses facing fluctuating demand set their capacity to meet peak demand, capacity will be underutilized during the off-peak period. There are a number of options available to improve business in off-peak periods, as discussed in earlier chapters, such as yield management or pricing strategies. In addition, capacity information and reporting can assist management in making decisions where there is fluctuating demand.[19]

Cooper and Kaplan offer and evaluate three possible solutions for recognizing the cost of unused capacity:[20]

1. *Ignore unused capacity.* Divide committed cost for the year by capacity utilized during that year. Every unit is therefore allocated the same amount of cost, which implies that the committed cost per unit provided during the low-volume period is the same as the

committed cost per unit in the high-volume period. This ignores the underlying economic reality that the business is well utilized in the high-volume period and only partially utilized in the low-volume period.

2. *Charge unused capacity costs to the low-volume period.* This calculates two unit rates for the committed costs, whereby the low-volume period has a higher unit cost than the high-volume period. This has a peculiar interpretation, where a higher price should be charged to dispose of the higher cost production in the low-volume season and a lower price in the high-volume season.
3. *Charge unused capacity costs to the high-volume period.* The implication here is that the reason why capacity is unused in the low-volume period is because of capacity required to cater to the high-volume period. Thus, the cost of unused capacity that the low-volume period is forced to carry is appropriately charged to the high-volume period.[21]

Applying Capacity Concepts

While the capacity concepts outlined previously may be interesting, much lies in their application. Let us contemplate the application of these ideas to a restaurant business.

Assuming that the number of seats available is the reference point for capacity, the starting point is the number of seats that fit the space available. How do you specify that? It is necessary to keep thoroughfares clear and to ensure that fire regulations are met. Beyond that, you wish to avoid overcrowding to ensure comfortable dining. What is meant by "overcrowded" or by "comfortable"? This depends on your strategy for the restaurant, the target market segment, and the dining experience that potential customers seek. Customer preferences shape strategy and strategic positioning. A fashionable expensive restaurant would allow far more space between chairs and tables than an inexpensive, no-frills restaurant.

There is also a time dimension associated with capacity, for example, in the sense of output per hour and available hours per week. The capacity of a restaurant might be stated as 500 diners. This assumes a time period of an evening, a week, or something similar. Capacity can be increased by either adding additional resources or improving efficiencies. A restaurant can seat many people during the number of hours it is open, which means that its capacity should be measured by seat hours. This can also be affected by how many seats at a table can be occupied. For example, if the restaurant staff set up tables to seat two, four, and six people and a party of five occupies a table for six, one seat is "wasted" for the duration of the meal. Other influences on capacity are table turn and the efficiency of chefs and waiting staff. The strategic positioning of the restaurant again affects the impact of these factors. Think about the difference between an up-market restaurant on the San Francisco waterfront and an affordable family restaurant in the suburbs.

While cost management focuses on the reality of resource consumption, cost assignment aims to measure resource consumption in dollar terms. This enables you to relate the cost of resources consumed in your business to cost objects such as outputs produced. We elaborate on this in the next section.

Resource Consumption: Assigning Costs

Figure 5.7 shows two perspectives: the top perspective represents the process or activities and their consumption of resources to provide outputs, while the lower perspective is the cost model, which imputes dollar values to the physical process flow. Input prices allow us to obtain the resource dollar cost and the resource-driver dollar rate. The resource-driver dollar rate in turn assigns the resource dollar cost to activity cost pools. The

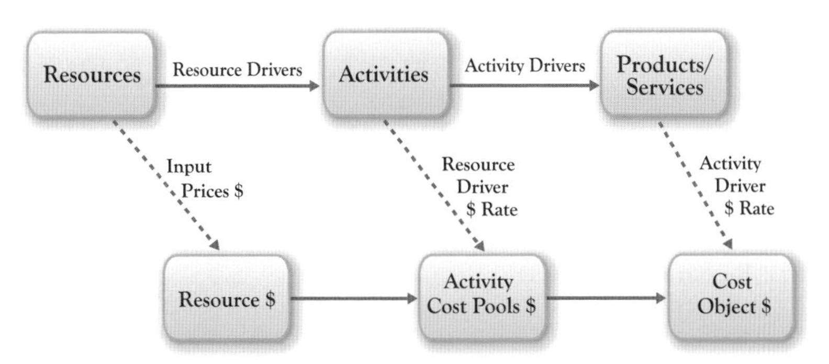

Figure 5.7. Physical service flows and dollar flows

activity-driver dollar rate provides the activity-based cost of the cost object (the product or service).

While Figure 5.7 illustrates a process-oriented view, we use a stronger cost model perspective in Figure 5.8. Figure 5.8 shows a two-stage process in which (a) the cost of resources consumed is assigned to activities, and (b) the cost of activities consumed is assigned to cost objects. Note that the two-stage process refers only to indirect costs, because the direct costs are traced directly to cost objects. Naturally, there are many complex issues concerning the choice and measurement of appropriate bases of assignment, including resource drivers (first stage) and activity drivers (second stage).

We explain Figure 5.8, which illustrates the process of cost assignment, as follows:

- The costs of resources are assigned to activities as opposed to departments. This recognizes that activities can cross departmental boundaries and are usually a better representation of the elements of the value chain than the organization structure.
- ABC uses drivers to assign costs, and the first-stage driver is a "resource driver." The purpose of this driver is to represent how resources are consumed by activities as opposed to simply allocating the cost. Examples of resource drivers are head count per activity to assign personnel costs, or number of square meters required per activity to assign occupancy costs. In the case of

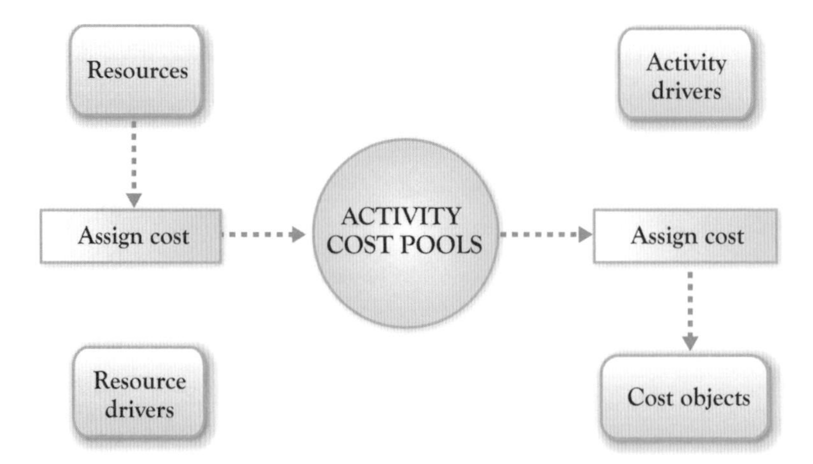

Figure 5.8. Cost assignment

a restaurant, this could be how much labor is required in the kitchen, what equipment is needed, utility usage, and the area required for the kitchen.
- Activity drivers are used to capture diversity of cost objects and, again, how each cost object consumes activities. There are usually several activity drivers in ABC related to the levels of the ABC hierarchy, including unit level, batch level, and product sustaining.

Alignment between activity drivers and cost drivers may be especially difficult (and also particularly important) in customer profitability analysis, which we cover in the next section.

Customer Profitability Analysis

Are difficult customers who are demanding, complaining, and constantly changing their requirements a problem or an opportunity? Businesses need to identify what it costs to service these customers and whether the customers are responding to the service strategy of the firm, or whether some of them are just being unreasonable. From a revenue management perspective, a necessary first step to deciding on actions to take is to know which customers are profitable and which are not. So why is customer profitability analysis (CPA) not more widely used?

Traditional accounting systems focus on product or service cost, with selling and administrative costs not included in unit cost. In particular, for financial reporting purposes, inventory valuation only includes product costs incurred in either manufacture or purchase. Consequently, the costs of other resources are excluded from profitability analysis. In addition, most accounting systems do not make it easy to identify costs relating to particular customers. This makes the analysis difficult to do and, more importantly, to justify doing. Nonetheless, various organizations have performed customer profitability analysis (CPA) over the years, with often surprising results. In one case, a firm discovered that, after taking the activity costs of servicing customers into account, 60% of its customers had a negative contribution.[22] Next, we provide some indications of costs associated with servicing customers' demands.[23]

We can recognize high-cost customers as those who

- require customized services;
- order in small quantities;
- order sporadically;
- require special delivery arrangements;
- frequently change order specifications;
- require manual processing;
- require considerable support;
- are slow to pay.

On the contrary, low-cost customers

- buy standard services;
- order in large quantities;
- order regularly;
- require standard delivery arrangements;
- do not change order specifications;
- require electronic processing;
- require little or no support;
- pay on time.

It is essential for service organizations to understand how customer characteristics drive activities and costs. We end this section with a mini case study of a travel agency, *Leisure Travel.*

Mini Case: Leisure Travel

Leisure Travel is a retail travel agency that focuses on holiday travel and on occasions, business trips. It has been in business for over 15 years, operating in a medium-sized suburb of a large city. Pressures on margins and increasing competition in recent years have eroded its profitability. June, the owner, is aware that the demands of customers on the agency's resources, principally the four travel consultants (including June), vary enormously. The average consultant cost per hour is $30, which allows for base pay, commissions, holiday and sick pay, and any relevant government taxes. June has compiled a file of two customers to see whether she can gain a better understanding of how to improve the profitability of her business. Table 5.5 provides details of each customer's use of the agency's resources.

Table 5.5. Use of agency resources by customers

	Mr. Ambrose	Ms. Brady
Initial contact	Telephone call 15 minutes	4 telephone calls; average 40 minutes each
Destination	Honolulu	Fiji
Length of trip	10 days	21 days
Number in party	2 adults, 1 child under 12	2 adults
Flight price	$700 per adult; $500 per child	$1, 246 per adult
Commission rates:		
Flights	6%	10%
Accommodation	10%	
Car hire		10%
Accommodation booked	Resort; $350 per night for 9 nights; no charge for child under 12	Booked initially for 20 nights then cancelled as decided to arrange own accommodation - consultant time 15 minutes
Car hire booked		Car rental; 21 days at $70 per day
Visit to office	1 visit; 40 minutes	4 visits; 20 minutes for each visit
Brochures	$15	$40
International telephone calls		$12 toll charge and 15 minutes time
Changes to bookings (average 15 minutes per change)	2 changes for flight bookings	10 changes for flight bookings and car rental dates
Other		Courier fees for expediting air tickets $40 - consultant time 20 minutes
Payment	Personal check	Credit card 1.5% charge by credit card company
Special discounts		Rewards card; discount 1%

It is obvious that Ms. Brady uses more resources than Mr. Ambrose. However, most travel agencies do not bother to quantify this, and, consequently, the additional costs and their effect on margins are overlooked. First, let us calculate the margins earned on each customer (see Table 5.6).

Although Mr. Ambrose generates slightly more commission in dollar terms than does Ms. Brady, the business that Ms. Brady has brought in is more profitable in terms of its margin percentage (i.e., 10.0% compared with 8.5%). But this is not the full story. Let us calculate the cost of

Table 5.6. Margins earned on customers

	Mr. Ambrose	Ms. Brady
Flights	$1,900.00	$2,492.00
Accommodation	$3,150.00	
Car		$1,470.00
Total revenue	$5,050.00	$3,962.00
Commission		
Flights	$114.00	$249.20
Accommodation	$315.00	
Car		$147.00
Total commission	$429.00	$396.20
Margin	8.5%	10.0%

consultants' time and expenses incurred in relation to each customer (see Table 5.7).

Our customer profitability analysis reveals that Mr. Ambrose is a better customer than Ms. Brady. Considering that June still has fixed costs to cover, she would prefer more customers like Mr. Ambrose and fewer like Ms. Brady. The gross margins based solely on commission led June to believe that Ms. Brady was a better customer than Mr. Ambrose. But before June decides not to deal with customers like Ms. Brady, there is a *caveat.*

Allied Stationery, a case study by John Shank, offers parallels to Leisure Travel. [24] The company introduces inventory management services to complement its business forms business. It differentiates a "commodity"

Table 5.7. Customer profitability analysis

	Mr. Ambrose	Ms. Brady
Consultant time (minutes)	85	440
Cost at $30 per hour	$42.50	$220.00
Brochures	$15.00	$40.00
Toll calls		$12.00
Courier fees		$40.00
Credit card charges		$59.43
Rewards card discount		$39.62
Total expenses	$57.50	$411.05
Customer contribution to fixed overheads	$371.50	($14.85)
Contribution	7.4%	-0.4%

product (business-forms stationery) from value-added services (inventory management of clients' business-forms needs). Given the details of two customers, the ABC system is applied to ascertain the cost of servicing each. The ordering profile of Customer X is straightforward, while that of Customer Y is complex, and this reflects low costs and profitability for Customer X and high costs and low profitability for customer Y. It seems that Allied Stationery should dump Customer Y and support Customer X. But if the company were to do that, they would be abandoning their differentiation strategy because Customer X does not use their special services and may at any time move to other suppliers in this business. On the other hand, Customer Y makes full use of Allied Stationery's services. At this point, Allied Stationery needs to decide what it can do to improve customer profitability.

As in the case of Customer Y (Allied Stationery), Leisure Travel is providing a service that meets Ms. Brady's expectations. There are other considerations, including the following:

- Consultants in the agency have the time to deal with Ms. Brady. While this may not always be the case, there is currently spare capacity, which means that they are not prevented from dealing with other customers.
- Ms. Brady may bring additional business, either as a repeat customer or by recommending the business to acquaintances.
- The customer contribution is negative but small. However, business from customers in this category is equally likely to prove marginally positive.
- There is a possibility of changing the behavior of customers such as Ms. Brady, thereby reducing the nonvalue-adding activities (e.g., expediting the tickets).

Summary

This chapter has covered considerable material in relation to cost systems and capacity management. We prefer ABC over other cost systems because it strongly connects with the activities of the organization, has direct links to an organization's value chain, and is able to distinguish resource consumption patterns. Cost drivers and the hierarchy of activities provide significant insights into resource consumption patterns. The cost drivers that call for specific attention are capabilities and capacity because of their potential effect on resource consumption. We have explained how these can be measured and reported as well as the issues involved. Information about the cost of unused capacity is particularly useful for revenue management when considering different pricing and yield strategies, especially in the capacity-management issues around seasonality or peak and off-peak periods. Finally, we have shown how customer profitability analysis can also assist revenue management through better understanding of which customers are profitable and which are not. Combining the results of customer profitability with knowledge of customer profiles can inform improved marketing and operational strategies.

Key Insights

- Revenue drivers and cost drivers underlie an organization's activities; they may affect one another, and you can influence them.
- Cost drivers and the hierarchy of activities influence resource consumption patterns; you can influence resource consumption by restructuring the business and redesigning processes.
- Activity-based costing enables you to measure revenue and the consumption of resources; you can manage revenue and costs with this information.
- Knowledge of unused capacity and its cost equips you with the ability to decide on alternative uses of, or a reduction in, that capacity; this helps you to achieve the right balance between cost and revenue.
- Even highly effective revenue management can result in losses if you do not ascertain and act on the profitability of customers.

CHAPTER 6
Performance Measurement

Show me the money.

—Jerry Maguire

Success in business means different things to different people. But when implementing a new revenue management system, we need to know how successful we have been in increasing revenues and improving our capacity management. We need a performance measurement system that measures the impact of what has been done, that evaluates that performance, and that determines what needs to happen in the future to ensure business goals are achieved.

This book has examined the various ways that service businesses can change their revenue management to be more successful, but change is pointless if you are unable to measure its effect. In this chapter, we examine the context in which performance measurement takes place and the performance indicators appropriate for service organizations. We also outline some analytical methods that can help businesses to answer the following fundamental performance questions that apply to revenue management or any other business activity that takes place:

- How well are we doing?
- What do we have to do to improve?
- Who are the "best-in-class" performers?

A Framework of Performance Measurement

Performance measurement is a key part of the performance management system (or management control system). The performance management system is necessary for aligning business activities with strategic goals. In large businesses, this is vital as the members of senior management are usually remote from the day-to-day operations and are unable to directly observe what is happening. However, even in smaller businesses, where most control is exercised through hands-on supervision, performance measurement is necessary for achieving success.

In designing a performance measurement system, we need to consider the context in which performance measurement takes place and how this affects what we mean by *performance* and *performance measurement.*

First, what do we mean by *performance*? While it seems almost unnecessary to ask, the idea of "performance" is complex. Often, it means different things to different people depending on their stake[1] in the business. For example, an owner might be interested in maximizing wealth through maximizing revenue and profit; an employee might be interested in how much physical work he or she performs; and customers might be interested in how satisfied they are with the services they purchase. So performance could be defined in terms of inputs (e.g., labor hours), outputs (e.g., revenue), or outcomes (e.g., customer satisfaction). In designing a performance measurement framework, we have to identify what type of performance a business needs to measure.

Next, what do we mean by *performance measurement*? This is often described as the comparison of results against expectations, with the assumption that continuous improvement is required. However, this definition has problems similar to *performance.* Whose performance do we want to measure, what are our expectations, and how are we going to measure and collect the right data to use? Further, to ensure fairness, we should take into account the impact of the environment. For example, a bank branch operating in a poor socioeconomic area is unlikely to be able to increase its revenue as much as one located in a rich area, and we should consider this when comparing the two banks' performances.

Getting the system right is only one part of the problem. We also need to consider how employees will respond to the system, that is, will it motivate them to focus on the right things, or will it provide them with opportunities to "game" the system, or will it lead to other dysfunctional behavior in either the selection or measurement of performance indicators? All this needs to be considered *before* implementing any new system.

A framework of performance measurement can help answer these questions by focusing management's attention on the individual processes within the business's value chain, the goals of the business, and the people who will be affected by the measurement process.

A basic performance measurement framework starts with the individual *activities* that consume *inputs* to produce *outputs*. This system should incorporate a feedback loop that *measures* and compares actual performance against *performance benchmarks*. Management can control the business by adjusting activities in response to the information generated from this system. Figure 6.1 illustrates this basic framework.

This simple framework may be suitable for a small business. However, it does not recognize the broader management system and business context. The management system will include related activities such as setting goals, planning, evaluating performance, and resource planning. In turn, the wider business context (including the business culture and the influence of its key stakeholders) influences these activities.

Figure 6.2 addresses these deficiencies by providing a comprehensive performance measurement framework. The all-pervading influence of the *business environment* at all levels of the performance management system is shown as the background shading in Figure 6.2. The requirements and expectations of key stakeholders will define this environment and its influence on performance measurement.

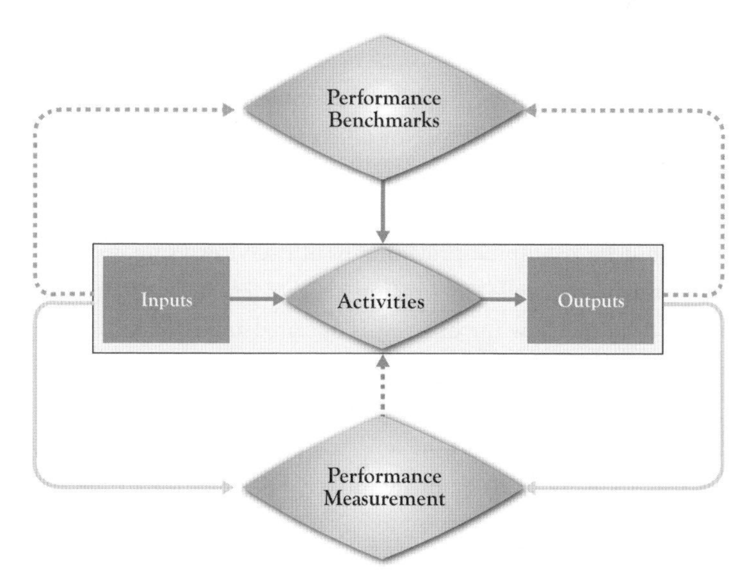

Figure 6.1. A simple performance measurement framework

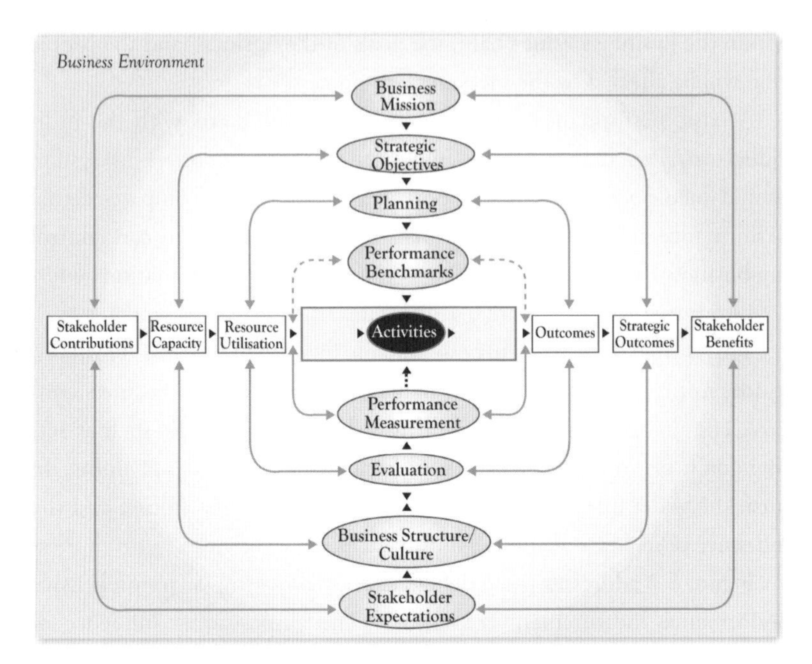

Figure 6.2. A comprehensive performance measurement system framework

Source: Rouse and Putterill (2003).

The outermost circle of this framework shows the relationship between the business and its *stakeholders' expectations*. Stakeholders include owners, employees, suppliers, customers, the government, and the general public. The influence of different stakeholder types will vary for different businesses and industries. For example, the general public is not likely to be influential for a privately owned software graphic design business, but for a hospital providing health services using government funding, the public could be a major stakeholder. Stakeholder expectations will influence how the business is operated and its vision and organizational goals.

The *vision* of the business is its response to stakeholder expectations (see Chapter 2). The vision is the long-term purpose of the business and sets out where it wants to be in the future. For example, a professional services firm could have the vision to be the best in the world. This *vision* determines the *strategic objectives* of the business, which are the business targets. So our services firm could have a strategic objective to increase its share of the Fortune 500 services market by 5% in the next year. It is these strategic objectives that influence the *planning* process, and they are the basis for generating *performance benchmarks*, often as part of the budgeting process.

The *strategic objectives* also determine the *strategic outcomes* of the business. These are a subset of the most important *outcomes* produced by the business. A business with strategic objectives related to revenue maximization is more likely to have strategic outcomes that emphasize pricing and capacity allocation. A business with a dominant professional culture is more likely to have strategic outcomes that emphasize technical outcomes.

Outcomes reflect the impact of *outputs* on stakeholder expectations. Business outcomes are more important than the outputs that generate them. Often, businesses fail to measure their outcomes, as they can be more difficult to identify than outputs. This is because outputs are the end result of a business process and can usually be measured in terms of the volume of the activity performed, for example, the number of meals served or the number of chargeable hours. Alternatively, outcomes—changes that occur as a result of the outputs produced—are harder to measure, for example, satisfied customers. However, as outcomes are closely linked to the benefits received by stakeholders, it is important that they are included in the measurement system. Otherwise, the business could be producing substantial outputs, but it may not contribute to the things stakeholders value. This, in turn, can lead to the withdrawal of stakeholder contributions and subsequent downsizing or failure of the business.

Stakeholder contributions are the resources (e.g., money, labor, or assets) that stakeholders give to the business in return for *benefits* received either directly (e.g., dividends, salaries) or indirectly (e.g., maintenance of a sustainable environment). These contributions are used to acquire *resource capacity* related to material, labor, and capital. These resources are utilized in the business to acquire *inputs* necessary for the business activities being measured.

Information on *resource utilization* and the level of *outcomes* can be used to measure the effectiveness and efficiency of the business. Effectiveness measures compare the level of outcomes to the level of outputs. Efficiency measures compare the level of outputs to the level of inputs.

Businesses need to have the appropriate resource capacity in place to pursue their strategic goals, as well as the capability to manage the business. In many service businesses, this resource capacity is people-related. This means that the *business culture* and *structure* will have a strong influence. For example, agreement on what the core competencies are will be influenced by whether the business has a flat or hierarchical structure. Similarly, whether the business is dominated by an individualistic or team-based business culture will influence how capacity is used.

The *business culture* and *structure* will also affect the *evaluation* of the results of the performance measurement. For example, in a hierarchical structure, there is more likely to be a formal budget-constrained evaluation process, with managers doing "everything by the book." In a flat structure, there is more likely to be a less-formal, profit-conscious process, with managers using both financial and nonfinancial information to determine performance.

The time horizon widens as you move from the center of Figure 6.2 to the outer circles, with activities near the center, such as setting performance benchmarks, occurring more frequently than activities on the outside, such as setting the business's vision. Importantly, each activity in this framework is part of a cascading relationship from the outside to the inside of the circle, such as from the strategic objectives to the performance benchmarks. Activities are also affected by other activities within the circle, such as from the strategic objectives to the strategic outcomes. Above all are the business's vision and its stakeholders' expectations. For this reason, the vision and stakeholders' expectations should be directly considered when identifying the right performance indicators to use in the measurement process.

Key Performance Indicators

There is truth in the old adage "what you measure, is what you get," so businesses need to be careful what they measure or they might not like the result. Businesses need to use performance indicators that measure the activities that contribute to the business achieving its strategy. Where performance measurement is concerned with revenue management, key performance indicators need to capture the impact of pricing strategies and the success in process improvements and capacity management.

For most businesses, a single indicator cannot capture the performance of all the key activities that lead to success. Businesses need to identify the most important value generation processes as well as monitor the key outcomes. Single performance measures are unlikely to do both. Even in private-sector businesses, where the maximization of the owners' wealth is paramount, it is necessary to capture the parts of the business process that will generate this wealth and that reflect other important stakeholders' expectations. Some of these measures are financial, such as return on sales (either gross or net profit divided by sales), and some are nonfinancial, such as customer satisfaction (measured using surveys or similar data collection tools).

Traditional performance indicators were primarily financial measures. This financial approach has been criticized because of its failure to reflect nonfinancial strategic objectives. Financial performance indicators have also been criticized because they often lack timeliness and can provide only a "snapshot" of performance. More importantly, a sole focus on financial ratios can lead management to focus only on the short term and fail to consider measures that capture the value creation linkages in the business.

The failure of financial performance measures has led to a number of performance models being developed. These frameworks link both financial and nonfinancial performance measures to objectives, strategy, and the competitive position of organizations.[2] The major advantage of incorporating nonfinancial performance indicators into a performance measurement system is that they can provide better information about future performance, whereas the focus of many financial indicators is past performance. Merchant and Van der Stede[3] argue that some nonfinancial performance indicators—such as customer satisfaction, product development, and product quality—are value drivers and, therefore, can be used as leading indicators to ensure managers are not short-term focused. Further, the use of performance indicators that model cause-and-effect relationships between activities and strategic objectives are more likely to ensure that the desired financial outcomes are achieved. However, nonfinancial performance indicators are not without problems, the most important being the cost of collecting the information, as these measures are not usually collected by the accounting information system. For example, measures of customer satisfaction require market survey data to be collected. Further, nonfinancial measures require judgment in both their identification and their measurement and, as a result, tend to be susceptible to manipulation. However, despite the potential cost and subjectivity of nonfinancial measures, research suggests that where a business operates in a complex and uncertain business environment, nonfinancial measures are a necessity. Conversely, where there is a low level of complexity and uncertainty in the business, such measures are likely to be less important in ensuring that a business accomplishes its strategic objectives.[4]

One of the most popular models for collating financial and nonfinancial performance indicators is the balanced scorecard (BSC), introduced by Kaplan and Norton.[5] The BSC incorporates multiple financial and nonfinancial performance indicators. These measures are grouped into four perspectives related to financial concerns, customer concerns, internal processes, and learning and growth. The BSC provides a more complete view of performance than single measures or multiple financial measures. The *financial* perspective focuses on key financial performance measures—for example, return on equity—and reports on the results of the business. The *customer* perspective focuses on how customers view the business and measures what is valued by them, such as customer satisfaction. The *internal processes* perspective focuses on the business's core competencies and includes measures of the efficiency of business processes, such as chargeable hours for a professional services firm. The *learning and growth* perspective focuses on continuous improvement and value creation, such as the number of successful new products or the level of staff training.

The BSC provides a focusing mechanism for identifying key performance indicators. However, the measures selected should reflect cause-and-effect relationships within the business. Kaplan and Norton[6] developed *strategy maps* as a tool for ensuring that the measures selected reflect the key cause-and-effect relationships between the four BSC perspectives, the business's strategy, and its value creation processes. The strategy map provides a visual representation of the relationships between each performance measure and shows how improvements in one will lead to improvements in another. For example, an airline with a strategic objective to be the preferred choice for business travelers might link improvements in its knowledge of what business travelers want (learning and growth) with improvements in business-class service (internal processes). This improved service could be linked with business traveler satisfaction (customer) and this, in turn, could be linked to increased revenue from business travelers (financial).

These cause-and-effect relationships mirror the relationships between the business's *critical success factors* and key performance indicators. Critical success factors are the factors that lead to the business meeting its strategic objectives and being successful. For example, building the brand reputation is likely to be a critical success factor for a hotel, as improvements are likely to lead to more people staying in the hotel and paying higher room rates. Key performance indicators related to this critical success factor could include measures of hotel capacity utilization and average room rates.

The BSC is not the only mechanism for selecting multiple performance indicators that capture the critical success factors of the business. Fitzgerald et al[7] developed a similar multidimensional model for measuring the performance of service businesses, as shown in Figure 6.3. This model incorporates six dimensions of performance, divided between performance indicators that measure the results of a business's strategy (competitiveness and financial performance measures) and factors that lead to strategic success (quality, flexibility, resource utilization, and innovation measures). As with the BSC, it is critical that the measures selected capture the elements of performance related to the critical success factors.

Key Performance Indicators for Service Businesses

Some performance indicators used in service businesses will be unique to this business segment, as they reflect the intangible nature of services and their perishability. Revenue management researchers[8] have suggested that revenue

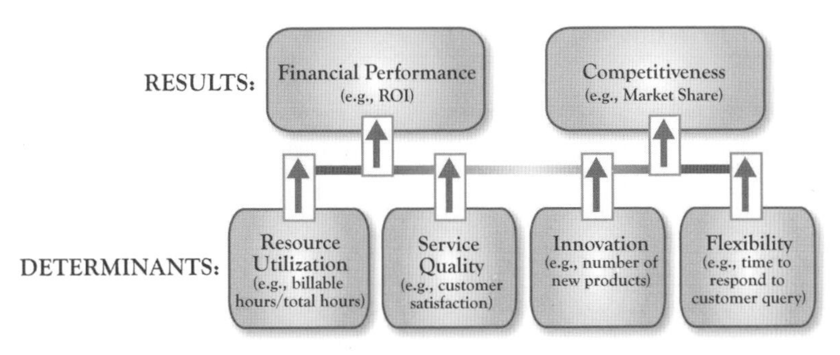

Figure 6.3. Fitzgerald et al.'s performance dimensions for service businesses

per available seat hour (*RevPASH)* provides a better measure of service performance than traditional financial measures, as it combines a measure of average revenue, such as revenue per seat, with a measure of capacity utilization, such as aircraft loadings. This measure has been used successfully in airlines, hotels, and restaurants, and it could potentially apply to any service business where average revenue and capacity measures are already captured.

The performance indicators shown in Table 6.1 relate to a restaurant chain located in San Francisco. Capacity utilization tells us how successful each restaurant is at attracting customers, and Fisherman's Wharf appears to be the best performer. Revenue per customer tells us something about how successful the restaurant is at pricing its services, and Presidio Heights appears to be the best performer. The problem is that neither measure on its own is sufficient and, taken together, the two ratios provide different rankings of performance. RevPASH combines both capacity and revenue and provides a better indicator of the revenue-generating performance of each restaurant. RevPASH shows that, overall, the Union Square restaurant is managing both capacity and pricing the best.

Capacity utilization and revenue per unit of capacity are closely entwined. Managers of service businesses need to consider these together in order to effectively manage performance. In restaurants, pricing can be actively managed to expand demand, such as by offering special menu promotions, or to shift peak-period demand to periods of low demand, such as by offering early-bird specials. These strategies are relatively common in restaurants. Managing capacity, however, is more difficult, as it involves not only how many tables and seats are available but also how long customers occupy those tables. Fixed seating configurations, such as booths, will lead

Table 6.1. Restaurant RevPASH

Restaurant	Average utilization	Average revenue per customer	RevPASH
Downtown	80%	$40.00	$32.00
Union Square	90%	$42.00	$37.80
Fisherman's Wharf	95%	$30.00	$28.50
North Beach	75%	$35.00	$26.25
Presidio Heights	70%	$45.00	$31.50
Russian Hill	80%	$40.00	$32.00
Mission District	65%	$35.00	$22.75

to unused capacity, where the number of customers eating together cannot be matched to the right-sized table. For example, four people allocated to a table that seats six immediately results in a two-seat loss of capacity for the duration of that meal. More flexible seating arrangements—such as bar counters, shared tables, or moveable tables—can help reduce this problem, but this requires employees to be more organized and customers to be more accepting. The length of each customer's meal also affects restaurant capacity utilization, as it will contribute to how many times a table can be used during the day. In chain restaurants, which have standard menus and relatively fast service, the meal duration is relatively quick and capacity is well utilized. In contrast, in a boutique restaurant, the meal is often designed to be a leisurely experience, with frequent changes expected to the food and wine menus. Customers will pay more for this leisurely experience, but the longer the meal duration, the fewer customers the restaurant can serve.

Where do the numbers come from? RevPASH (revenue per available seat hour) combines two ratios:

$$\text{Revenue per customer} = \frac{\text{total revenue}}{\text{number of customers served}}$$

$$\text{Capacity utilization percentage} = \frac{\text{number of customers served}}{\text{total capacity}}$$

$$\text{RevPASH} = \text{revenue per customer} \times \text{capacity utilization \%}$$

$$\text{Or: RevPASH} = \frac{\text{total revenue}}{\text{total capacity}}$$

RevPASH, which is often used in restaurants, means "revenue per available seat hour." Other variations include

RevPAR = revenue per available room-night (hotels)

RevPSM = revenue per available seat mile (airlines)

RevPAC = revenue per available cabin (cruise ships)

RevPAST = revenue per available space for a given time (convention centers)

RevPATT = revenue per available tee time (golf courses)

RevPASH measures tend to be specific to particular businesses, reflecting industry measures of revenue and capacity. There are, of course, many other measures needed to develop the type of performance management system shown in Figure 6.2. As discussed previously, the selection of these measures needs to capture both the wider business context and the particular business's critical success factors. These will differ for each business. Figure 6.4 shows an illustrative BSC for a generic service business pursuing a revenue management strategy. The list of measures used is not exhaustive, and we have included not only RevPASH but also its constituent parts, revenue per customer and capacity utilization. Reviewing all three together will enable a business not only to identify the level of performance but also to decompose that performance into success in relation to pricing and capacity utilization.

Performance Analysis Methods

Multiple performance measures are very useful in measuring different aspects of performance, but they can create problems. Most people struggle to cope with more than a few measures, particularly when measures provide different rankings of performance. The more measures included in the performance measurement system, the bigger the problem, as

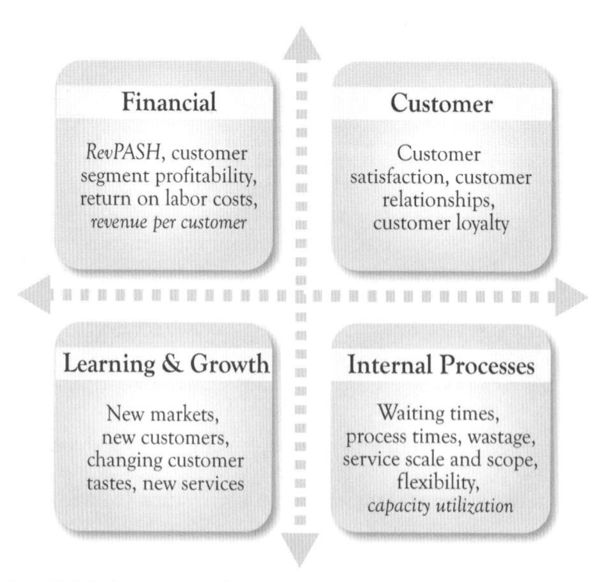

Figure 6.4. BSC for service businesses

managers are unable to use those measures to provide an overall view of how well the business is doing. In addition, most managers tend to be functionally fixated, that is, the accountant focuses on the financial measures, the marketing manager focuses on the customer measures, the operations manager on the internal processes measures, and the marketing, human resources, and IT managers on various learning and growth measures related to their particular domains. Further, managers often have favorite measures that get fossilized in the system, because managers will not give up their favorite, regardless of any decline in its usefulness. Lastly, while employees and managers might share the same vision for the business, they often are unable to agree on the relative importance of different strategic objectives, and this, in turn, is reflected in how they view the relative importance of performance measures.

To address these problems, the performance measurement system needs to be able to balance the measures in a way that identifies the overall level of performance, the things needed to improve performance, and best practice. One way of doing this is by using formal methods of performance analysis. We outline two alternate methods that help to balance the measures and provide insights into performance that are not always obvious from looking at multiple measures. The first, a performance measurement index, is relatively simple to use. The second, data envelopment analysis (DEA), is more complex but provides more information about how to improve performance.

Performance Measurement Index

The performance measurement index, as described by Lee,[9] is a simple and cost-effective method of combining multiple performance measures. The method involves the following steps:

1. Identify the performance areas to be measured. There is no limit to the number that can be included, but as discussed, the areas should reflect critical success factors. If you include too many performance areas, the important measures can get lost in the detail. We suggest limiting the number of performance areas from 3 to 10.
2. Identify performance measures for each area. The measures selected for each area should reflect cause-and-effect relationships. If the area

is product quality, the measure should capture the most important aspects of product quality.

3. Design a performance index that lists each performance area and the related performance measures.
4. Assign the same scale to each performance measure—such as 0 to 10 or 0 to 100 or 0 to 5—depending on the level of variability in the measures you want to capture.
5. Identify the value of the measure that represents the best performance, most likely (or normal) performance, and worst performance. These levels represent targets for each measure.
6. Assign a value in the scale to these three targets. For example, for a scale of 0 to 10, the best performance will be assigned a value of 10; the most likely performance, a value of 5; and the worst performance, a value of 0.
7. Assign values of the measure to the rest of the scale. This process is flexible, and both linear and nonlinear relationships for the measures can be represented by the scale. Negative values for measures can also be included, although are likely to be assigned values at the low end of the scale where they represent poor performance. The process of assigning measure values to the scale values is subjective but should reflect the overall range of possible results.
8. Assign a weight to each performance area that represents its importance to the overall strategic objectives of the business. The total weights assigned should equal 100% in order to preserve the scale used.
9. Record actual performance for each measure for the period under review (or for the business unit being evaluated), and use the performance index to calculate an overall performance score.

As an example, Galveston Seaside Hotel has identified four performance areas and associated measures that it believes are related to its critical success factors, as shown in Table 6.2. These areas are customers (measured by customer satisfaction), financial results (measured by RevPAR, revenue per available room night), business growth (measured by sales growth), and internal processes (measured by room occupancy rates). The hotel has developed an index that identifies the worst, most likely, and best

Table 6.2. Galveston Seaside Hotel Performance Measurement Index

Performance targets	Index	Customer satisfaction	RevPAR	Sales growth	Room occupancy
Best	10	100%	$220	15%	90%
	9	96%	$215	12%	88%
	8	92%	$210	9%	86%
	7	88%	$200	7%	84%
	6	84%	$190	5%	82%
Most likely	5	80%	$180	3%	80%
	4	75%	$170	2%	77%
	3	70%	$165	1%	74%
	2	65%	$160	0%	70%
	1	60%	$155	-1%	65%
Worst performance	0	55%	$150	-5%	60%
Weighting		30%	30%	20%	20%

performance targets for each measure and has assigned values of 0, 5, and 10, respectively. For example, a customer satisfaction score of 100%, where all customers are happy with the service, is the best the hotel expects to get and it is assigned a score of 10. Next, the hotel assigned values of the measures for the rest of the 0-to-10 scale. Finally, through discussions with the managers and key employees, a subjective weighting for each performance area has been agreed on. They believe this weighting reflects the relative importance of each area in accomplishing the hotel's mission.

The hotel wants to determine its performance over 3 months in 2010, has collected data in relation to each measure, and has used this to calculate the performance score. The performance index for each month is calculated by comparing the actual results to the matching scale shown in Table 6.2. This calculation is shown in Table 6.3.

Table 6.3. Galveston Seaside Hotel Monthly Performance

Month	Customer satisfaction		RevPAR		Sales growth		Room occupancy		Performance index
	Actual	Index	Actual	Index	Actual	Index	Actual	Index	
April	96%	9	$200	7	1%	3	84%	7	6.8
May	92%	8	$200	7	0%	2	86%	8	6.5
June	88%	7	$210	8	2%	4	88%	9	7.1

The Lee[10] method is a cost-effective, flexible, and reasonably easy method of combining multiple measures, but it has some limitations. First, it is only practical when you have a small number of measures. Second, it requires a lot of subjective judgment to be made in setting the target levels of performance, the scales to assign to the performance measure values, and the weights to apply to each performance area. Last, the method uses a fixed set of weights to apply to each performance area. This may not be a problem when comparing time periods for the same business and when the nature of the business has not changed. But if you are comparing multiple business units, such as hotels in a hotel chain, then the managers of each hotel could disagree on the relative weights because the critical success factors for each hotel vary.

Data Envelopment Analysis

An alternative performance analysis method that allows for varying weights to apply to different performance measures is DEA. DEA calculates efficiency scores (with 100% representing best practice) for each business unit being analyzed. It also provides target values for each unit to improve performance and it identifies best-in-class performers. The advantage with using DEA combined with revenue management is that these target values can be expressed in terms of increases in outputs, consistent with the goal of revenue maximization.

The foundation of DEA is the production process, which consumes inputs (*X*) to produce outputs (*Y*), as shown in Figure 6.5.

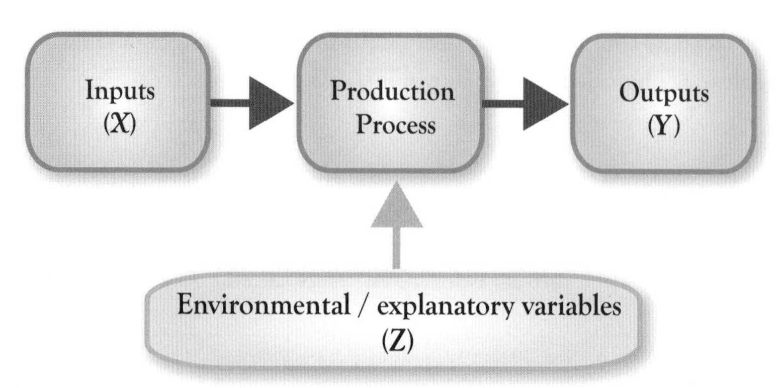

Figure 6.5. The production process

Efficiency scores are measured for a group of similar business or production units whose performance we want to compare. These units are called decision-making units (DMUs) and could be, for example, a group of retail stores in a retail chain, a group of bank branches, or a group of hotels in a hotel chain. Performance is measured in terms of how much output (*Y*) a DMU can produce for the inputs (*X*) it uses, relative to the performance of the other DMUs being compared.

In some cases, not all business units operate in the same competitive environment, for example, retail stores in areas of high foot traffic versus those in areas of low traffic. DEA can "level the playing field" by adjusting efficiency scores to reflect these environmental or explanatory variables (*Z*). In this way, managers are only held accountable for the things they can control.

Figure 6.6 shows seven DMUs (A to G) producing a single output, using a single input. DMUs that produce high amounts of output (e.g., C) generally use more input than DMUs that produce low amounts of output (e.g., A). However, which of these DMUs is performing best?

Look at E, which uses about the same amount of input as C but produces much less output. Clearly, C's performance is better than E's. That is, E is dominated by C, and the amount of inefficiency (in terms of outputs) is shown by the vertical line from E to C. This is the *output orientation* because performance is defined in terms of the amount of additional output that could be produced for the same amount of input. Using the output orientation in DEA will provide output targets for inefficient DMUs that will promote the maximization of revenue in each business unit.

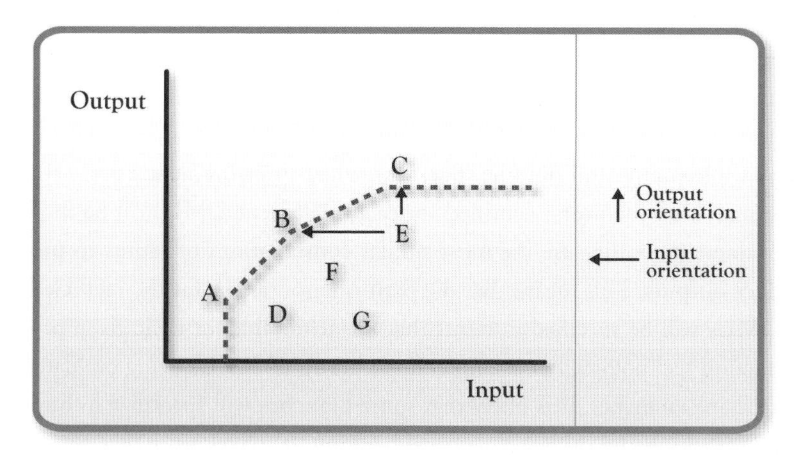

Figure 6.6. Single input-output process

An alternative perspective is provided by the *input orientation.* Look at B, which produces about the same level of output as E but uses much less input. E is dominated by B, and the amount of inefficiency (in terms of inputs) is shown by the horizontal line from E to B. This input orientation specifies performance in terms of the reduction in inputs that is possible while still producing the same amount of output. Generally, this view of performance will be less applicable for revenue management, although it can be relevant when looking at process improvements in markets where increases in output (and revenue) are difficult to achieve.

Looking at all the DMUs in Figure 6.6, we can see that DMUs A, B, and C are the best performers because there are no other DMUs that either produce more output for the same amount of input (output orientation) or produce the same amount of output using less input (input orientation). We call the line between these DMUs the *efficiency frontier.* This represents the best practice for the group of DMUs being compared. These efficient DMUs—A, B, and C,—have an efficiency score of 100% and they will provide the *performance peers* for the inefficient DMUs (D, E, F, and G). The inefficient DMUs will have efficiency scores of less than 100%. Improvement targets can be calculated for each inefficient DMU in terms of either reductions in inputs (input orientation) or expansion of outputs (output orientation).

As mentioned, for revenue management, the output orientation is likely to be the most appropriate performance perspective for identifying the level of inefficiency and the target levels of output expansion that will result in revenue maximization. In a single input-single output example, the identification of the best performers is not difficult, and the use of DEA to determine the efficient and inefficient DMUs is not really necessary. However, one of the strengths of DEA is that it can combine multiple inputs and outputs. Further, process improvement using DEA ensures that the peers identified for each inefficient DMU will be those business units that use the most similar combinations of inputs to produce outputs. This means that the performance targets for the inefficient DMUs will be specified in terms that are achievable for their given production technology. For example, if the group of DMUs being evaluated are bank branches, it is likely that some branches will specialize in business banking and others in personal banking. It makes sense that performance targets for inefficient branches should reflect their own particular business combination. Sending the branch manager of an inefficient suburban branch to visit the manager of an efficient downtown branch is unlikely to lead to significant process improvements.

DEA efficiency scores can be calculated using commercial software,[11] which will produce performance data similar to the example shown in Table 6.4. This table shows performance data for DMU E from our previous example. The information details the efficiency score of 75%, calculated assuming constant returns to scale (CRS) and using an output orientation. CRS assumes that an increase in inputs will result in proportionately the same increase in outputs. The peer units for E are identified (DMU C), together with the target increase in outputs required to improve E's performance to 100%.

Table 6.4 shows that DEA provides answers to the questions we posed at the start of this chapter:

- How well are we doing? This is measured by the efficiency scores.
- What do we have to do to improve? This is provided by the performance targets.
- Who are the "best-in-class" performers? This is provided by the performance peers.

The example provided here is simple, but as mentioned, DEA is able to combine multiple inputs and outputs to generate a single efficiency score. We presented results assuming CRS, but alternative specifications of DEA are available that will incorporate variable returns to scale. The inputs and outputs can be measured using a variety of measures, and price and cost data are not required to calculate the efficiency scores, although they can be used.

Table 6.4. Example of DEA Performance Data

DMU name	E
Orientation	Output
CRS efficiency score	75%
Peer unit(s)	C
Actual input	200
Actual output	100
Target input	200
Target output	134

Where do the numbers come from? DEA is an application of linear programming. The constant returns-to-scale model first proposed by Charnes, Cooper, and Rhodes[12] is specified in its envelopment form, output orientation:

$$\text{maximize } \theta$$
$$\textit{subject to:}$$
$$\sum_{j=1}^{n} y_{rj}\lambda_j \geq \theta y_{ro} \qquad r=1,\ldots,s$$
$$\sum_{j=1}^{n} x_{ij}\lambda_j \leq x_{io} \qquad i=1,\ldots,m$$
$$\lambda_j \geq 0, \qquad j=1,\ldots,n$$
$$\theta_0 \text{ unrestricted}$$

For a group of n DMUs that use a combination of m inputs (x) to produce s outputs (y), the linear program finds the maximum value of θ for each DMU that provides it with the highest possible efficiency score. The linear program is solved n times, once for each DMU, and θ can take any value from 1 to infinity with $1/\theta$ equal to the efficiency score for each DMU being examined (DMU0). The λ values are the proportion of the units on the frontier that are the peers for the inefficient DMUs. For a 100% efficient DMU, λ will be equal to 1 for that DMU's inputs and outputs and 0 for all other DMUs. That is, for an efficient DMU, it is its only peer.

DEA and Process Improvement

The core of DEA is the production process and the consumption of inputs to produce outputs. This view is essentially the same as used in activity-based costing (ABC) and activity-based management (ABM), which look at how the activities necessary to produce cost objects (outputs) are related to resource (input) consumption. The main difference is that DEA uses aggregated data about inputs and outputs, whereas ABC disaggregates data to focus on the links between activities, resources, and cost objects. Figure 6.7 illustrates this relationship. Rouse, Harrison, and

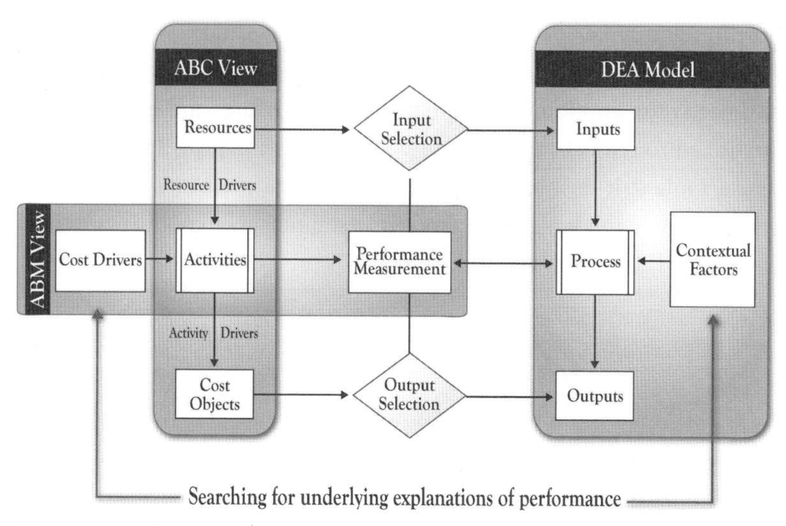

Figure 6.7. Activity-based costs and management and DEA

Diagram adapted from Rouse, Harrison, and Turner (2010).

Turner[13] describe how using DEA efficiency scores can reveal relationships between activities and resource usage that can provide additional insights into process improvement, not identifiable simply from the use of ABC or ABM alone.

For this reason, the use of DEA (output orientation), together with ABC, can assist in the successful implementation of revenue management strategies. Together, DEA and ABC can help a business focus on its pricing strategies to increase its revenue, while at the same time implementing process improvements to reduce resource usage and better allocate resources between activities.

Summary

Performance measurement is an integral part of revenue management. Without the ability to measure and evaluate the impact of revenue management, it is impossible to determine whether we have been successful. This process means more than just measuring increases in revenue, as this is only part of the revenue management cycle. If we fail to measure process improvements and capacity utilization, our performance measurement system is only telling, at best, half the story. In this chapter, we have looked at the context in which performance measurement takes place and how to identify key performance indicators. In addition, we identified a performance measure designed specifically for revenue management. We also noted the importance of using multiple measures and ensuring they are linked to critical success factors. Lastly, we have provided some analytical tools that enable us to combine multiple performance measures and to answer the key performance issues about how good we are, how we can get better, and who is the best.

Key Insights

- Performance measurement systems need to be designed in the context of the wider business environment and management control system.
- Multiple performance measures are likely to provide a better view of performance than single measures. However, these measures need to reflect the critical success factors of the business and should be based on cause-and-effect relationships.
- RevPASH provides a useful measure of success in revenue management, as it combines measures of capacity utilization and pricing.
- The use of multiple measures requires a method of analysis that allows us to combines these measures. We described two possible approaches—one relatively simple (the performance index) and the other, complex (DEA).
- Whichever performance analysis tool is selected for revenue management, it needs to provide management with the right information about pricing strategies, process improvements, and capacity utilization.

CHAPTER 7

Summary

Revenue management is a unifying approach for many activities performed by an organization in the pursuit of profit (or avoidance of loss in the case of not-for-profits). On a strict revenue perspective, it aims to improve an organization's performance by getting the best revenue streams possible from its resources. Focusing, however, on revenue by itself is not sufficient. It is critical to balance revenue initiatives with managing processes and resources. Increasing revenue at the cost of higher expenses or investment can be counterproductive. This is why we have described not only revenue maximizing methods but also ways in which processes and activities can be better managed. We believe that most organizations can benefit from revenue management. In this book, we have shown you how to apply new techniques and gain insights for improving revenue flows while controlling costs and investment.

New ideas and technologies are changing the world of business on a daily basis, and revenue management is no exception. By now, most of us have experienced dynamic pricing in some form or other, either through Internet markets, such as eBay, or through particular suppliers, such as the airlines. Some organizations such as Amazon have been suspected of offering different prices for the same product (e.g., DVDs per Computerworld[1]) using their collected history of past customer preferences and purchasing behavior to tailor prices to individual customers. Certainly, Amazon is very good at suggestive selling, with regular messages concerning products that are similar to past purchases. Weiss and Mehotra[2] note a rumor that Coca-Cola has been testing vending machines that will adjust their prices in response to changes in temperature. Since these machines do not seem to have been introduced, one can only surmise that Coca-Cola decided not to pursue this direction on the basis of potential consumer resistance. On the process management side, organizations have been improving their methods here as well. Our favorite is the clever capacity management approach used by Disney in its theme parks. The following extract from their website provides a quick explanation of how it works:[3]

> How does FastPass work?
>
> Each FastPass attraction will have two displays of time
>
> The first display of time will give guests the approximate waiting time if you were to enter the attraction right then.
>
> The second display of time indicates the window of time for a return visit if you were to get a FastPass right then.
>
> If the wait is acceptable then go ahead and enjoy the attraction. If the wait is longer than you feel is reasonable then go ahead and get a FastPass for a return appointment to enjoy the attraction later.

This clever use of technology and capacity management provides greater value for customers as well as better use of the theme park's resource capacity. Other more analytical changes include more sophisticated methods for yield management. Walczak, Mardan, and Kallesen[4] describe how data envelopment analysis (Chapter 6) can be combined with expected marginal seat revenue, or EMSR (Chapter 3) to identify efficient fare classes. Ng[5] examines the future of pricing and revenue models in four areas.

- First, we need to understand how including the customer and other stakeholders for co-creation (refer to willingness to pay in Chapter 1) could impact on pricing.
- Second, there will be multiple stakeholders contributing to and gaining from a complex service system with pricing adjusting to the dynamics of the system.
- Third, we do not all need to own a tool or product that we only use two or three times a year. Ng argues that we will move toward a pricing system based on rights to use as opposed to ownership. Ng argues that when customers rent or buy, they are buying outcomes as opposed to the goods or services themselves.
- Finally, we need to recognize the context in which consumers use goods and services and price according to each context.

> Ng argues that "Future pricing models will be more concerned with not just who the customers are but how they derive their value in-use, that is, when, where and how customers are consuming the goods and activities."

So what are the directions that revenue management is moving toward in the future? We shall indulge in some crystal-ball speculation based upon current trends and research directions.

In the preface to this book, we referred to the *OECD Observer*[6] and OECD report[7] that indicated that services comprise 70% of total employment and value-added[8] in OECD countries. We believe this percentage will remain high and possibly increase as manufacturing organizations adopt a stronger focus on service. Given the revenue management focus on services, its influence can only grow to match the large number of service organizations for which it has so much to offer.

No speculative view of the future would be complete without mention of technology, especially information-processing technology. The proliferation of computing power enables the smallest organization to perform sophisticated analyses that would only have been possible on large mainframe computers 30 years ago. We have referred to some of these more complex methods—such as EMSR, linear programming, and project management—throughout this book. There are many more methods of greater sophistication, but the good news is that most of them can be run on the ordinary personal computer. Data collection is always an issue, and most readers would recognize the difficulties in collecting the data quantities required to apply some of the methods we have described. But even data collection is increasingly facilitated by machines that automatically record customer details, times, and quantities at the point of sale. This technology is increasingly available for small to medium-sized organizations, thus enabling revenue management to extend both horizontally across organizations and vertically in terms of size.

The other major influence will be the growth of service science management. Led by IBM, this is a global development program that combines universities, industry, and governments in a common ground of service performance and innovation. The goal is to apply scientific knowledge to the design and improvement of service systems for business and societal purposes (such as efficiency, effectiveness, and sustainability). Underpinning service science is service-dominant logic, which is explained as follows:

> Service-Dominant (S-D) logic presents its message through ten foundational premises. In brief, these premises put the following concepts to the fore: service is the fundamental basis of exchange. Note that it is "service" and not "services" as opposed to goods; goods are merely distribution mechanisms of service. Operant resources are those which do something to something. Both businesses and customers are operant resources meaning that they both act as opposed to the mainstream marketing idea that suppliers do things to customers who just react. The customer is always a co-creator of value. A supplier can only offer a value proposition on the market; the value actualization is performed by users in an idiosyncratic and contextual way. The network aspect is implicit through the statement that all social and economic actors are resource integrators, implying that value creation takes place through interaction in complex networks. S-D logic is based on international findings and openness to continuous improvements and creative developments.[9]

Co-creation will become an increasing fact of life for most organizations, and systems and processes will need to be designed to manage this interface between internal and external actors. In reality, this interface may become seamless, and many organizations have already commenced this journey in their new product development activities under the heading of "open innovation."

These are a few descriptions of possible future directions. We hope that you will explore these in the respective journals listed in the references, especially those journals that focus on revenue management. The remainder of this chapter contains the key insights provided at the end of each chapter for easy reference.

Chapter 2 Key Insights

- Understand your organization's environment and context. Use the available tools to analyze an organization's environment.

   - Start with a SWOT (strengths, weaknesses, opportunities, and threats) analysis—it is easy to do and always provides insights.
   - Use Porter's industry analysis to analyze the external environment in which your organization operates.
   - Identify your existing core competences. Later, you can identify if you need to develop new ones.
- Use Porter's competitive positioning or the blue ocean tools to identify what you should do. (We favor blue ocean, but Porter's model can still be seen in operation in many organizations.)
- Use the strategic elements depicted in Figure 2.1 to formulate your strategy or to evaluate your current strategy.
- Embed revenue management in the strategy from the objectives and planning to the detailed policies.
- Communicate and obtain buy-in from employees. This is *the* critical success factor. Processes like the search conference can overcome resistance and inertia while ensuring that communication and buy-in are achieved.

Chapter 3 Key Insights

- Strategic pricing (demand-based pricing) links the prices charged to the features that customers value rather than the cost of creating a product or service.
- Yield management uses strategic pricing to maximize revenue by charging customer segments prices that approximate the highest prices they are willing to pay.
- Customers can be segmented by identifying sorting mechanisms that group customers with similar requirements and willingness to pay. The sorting mechanisms used must be capable of keeping customer groups separate so that high-price customers are not converted into low-price customers.
- Various yield management techniques are available to allocate capacity to different customer segments in a way that maximizes revenue. These techniques range from the relatively simple, such as the threshold curve, to the more complex EMSR and linear programming methods.

- All yield management methods need accurate customer demand data to enable predictions to be made about future levels of demand for different groups of customers paying different prices.

Chapter 4 Key Insights

- Organization design is a major cost driver; pay attention to process relationships and reduce variability within a process as much as possible.
- Start with the "textbook" examples of nonvalue-added activities (NVA) and then consult your customers to identify your specific NVA.
- The bottleneck sets the rate of throughput (i.e., revenue and expenses) and is the primary focus for improving processes and revenue.
- Project manage the process! You will understand the flows better, and there are well-established project management tools that provide insights for improving resource usage.

Chapter 5 Key Insights

- Revenue drivers and cost drivers underlie the organization's activities; they may affect one another, and you can influence them.
- Cost drivers and the hierarchy of activities influence resource consumption patterns; you can influence resource consumption by restructuring the business and redesigning processes.
- Activity-based costing enables you to measure the consumption of resources and revenue; you can manage revenue and costs with this information.
- Knowledge of unused capacity and its cost equips you to decide on alternative uses of, or a reduction in, that capacity; this helps you to achieve the right balance between cost and revenue.
- Even highly effective revenue management can result in losses if you do not ascertain and act on the profitability of customers.

Chapter 6 Key Insights

- Performance measurement systems need to be designed in the context of the wider business environment and management control system.
- Multiple performance measures are likely to provide a better view of performance than single measures. However, these measures need to reflect the critical success factors of the business and should be based on cause-and-effect relationships.
- revenue per available seat hour (RevPASH) provides a useful measure of success in revenue management, as it combines measures of capacity utilization and pricing.
- The use of multiple measures requires a method of analysis that allows us to combines these measures. We described two possible approaches—one relatively simple (the performance index) and the other, complex (data envelopment analysis [DEA]).
- Whichever performance analysis tool is selected for revenue management, it needs to provide management with the right information about pricing strategies, process improvements, and capacity utilization.

Notes

Preface

1. Pilat (2005).
2. OECD (2005).

Chapter 1

1. Satariano (2010).
2. Cross (1997).
3. Many of us might think that nothing has changed!
4. Ekelund (1970).
5. Ramsay (2010).

Chapter 2

1. Steiner, Miner, & Gray (1986), p. 11.
2. Bartol & Martin (1991), p. 157.
3. Steiner, Miner, & Gray (1986), p. 16.
4. Adapted from Rouse (1997).
5. Porter (1980, 2008).
6. Cooper & Slagmulder (1997).
7. Strategic business units (SBUs) are distinct businesses within an organization—often characterized by product families—that can be managed independently of other businesses within the organization.
8. Feller, Shunk, & Callarman (2006).
9. Prahalad & Hamel (1990).
10. Prahalad & Hamel (1990).
11. Prahalad & Hamel (1990).
12. Kim & Mauborgne (2005).
13. Kim & Mauborgne (2010).
14. This would be the case unless you are the husband and insist on driving.
15. The material in this section is adapted from Rouse and Swales (2001).
16. The search conference method is accredited to Fred Emory and Eric Triss (Tavistock Institute, UK).

17. This is in opposition to a closed system, where no interactions are permitted between the system and its environment.

18. A good description of the process and a list of organizations that have used it (including Microsoft) can be found on this website: http://www.worldtrans.org/qual/searchconf.html

19. Miles & Snow (1978).

20. Coombs & Maguire wrote the Toulette's Stores case, which is based on a listed company (name and details altered).

21. The Argenti system sets out, in detail, the structure and process to which we refer briefly in this chapter, particularly in the Toulette's Stores case study. See http://www.argentisys.com/ accessed September 22, 2010.

22. Porter (1980, 2008).

Chapter 3

1. For a fuller discussion, see Porter (1998).
2. Evans & Berman (2010).
3. See Berry & Yadav (1996).
4. See Berry & Yadav (1996).
5. See Kimes (1989) or Weatherford & Bodily (1992) for a fuller discussion.
6. Littlewood (1972).

Chapter 4

1. Raffish & Turney (1991).
2. Hansen & Mowen (2009).
3. Baker (2002).
4. Porter (1985), p. 70.
5. Turney (1992), p. 20.
6. Stata (1989).
7. Goldratt & Cox (1992).
8. Goldratt & Cox (1992).

9. Usually it is more useful to exclude this, as the meal duration is actually the bottleneck as far as customers waiting for a table are concerned. Therefore, the waiting time is dependent on meal duration.

Chapter 5

1. Raffish & Turney (1991).
2. Turney (1992).
3. Shank & Govindarajan (1993).

4. Cooper & Kaplan (1999).
5. Maguire & Rouse (2004).
6. Stalk (1992).
7. Stalk (1992).
8. Teece, Pisano, & Shuen (1997).
9. Maguire & Heath (1997), p. 26.
10. Horngren, Datar, Foster, Rajan, & Ittner (2009).
11. Maguire & Heath (1997), p. 28.
12. Maguire & Heath (1997).
13. Gantt (1915).
14. Gantt (1915).
15. Maguire & Heath (1997).
16. Cooper & Kaplan (1999).
17. Maguire & Heath (1997).
18. Maguire & Heath (1997) illustrate this by reference to the Crown Cork and Seal case and the Coatings case found in Govindarajan & Shank (1989), and Maguire & Rouse (1994), respectively, both of which retained unused capacity in reserve for this purpose.
19. See Maguire & Cai (2003) for a comprehensive case study of these issues in relation to a commuter bus service.
20. Cooper & Kaplan (1999).
21. See Bernier & Cooper (1988) for a good illustration.
22. Bellis-Jones (1992).
23. Drawn from Cooper & Kaplan (1999).
24. Shank (1996).

Chapter 6

1. We refer to people who have a stake in a particular organization as stakeholders. Depending on the organization, and whether it is public, private, for profit, or not-for-profit stakeholders can include business owners, employees, customers, suppliers, the local community, and the IRS or other government bodies; for some organizations, it includes everyone.
2. See Kennerley & Neely (2002) for a discussion of the development of performance measurement frameworks.
3. Merchant & Van der Stede (2007).
4. See, for example, Govindarajan & Shank (1992).
5. Kaplan & Norton (1992, 1996).
6. Kaplan & Norton (2001).
7. Fitzgerald, Johnston, Brignall, Silvestro, & Voss (1991).
8. See, for example, Kimes (1999).
9. Lee (1992).

10. Lee (1992).

11. For example, Saitech DEA-Solver Pro, Performance Improvement Management DEAsoft or Banxia Frontier Analysis.

12. Charnes, Cooper, & Rhodes (1978).

13. See Rouse, Harrison, & Turner (2010).

Chapter 7

1. Rosencrance (2000).
2. Weiss & Mehotra (2001).
3. Disneyworld (2010).
4. Walczak, Mardan, & Kallesen (2010).
5. Ng (2010).
6. Pilat (2005).
7. OECD (2005).
8. "Value-added" is being used in a different sense here than in Chapter 4 in that it refers to the increase in economic value of goods and services produced in an economy over and above the cost of materials or brought-in supplies.
9. Barile, Spohrer, & Polese (2010).

References

The Argenti System of Strategic Planning. http://www.Argentisys.com. Accessed September 22, 2010.

Baker, W. (2002). Eliminate non-value-added costs. *Industrial Management 44*(3), 22–27.

Barile, S., Spohrer, J., & Polese, F. (2010). System thinking for service research advances. *Service Science, 2*(1/2), i–iii.

Bartol, K. M., & Martin, D. C. (1991). *Management.* New York, NY: McGraw-Hill.

Bellis-Jones, R. (1992). Activity-based cost management. In C. Drury (Ed.), *Management accounting handbook* (100–127). Oxford, England: Butterworth-Heinemann, in association with CIMA.

Bernier, M., & Cooper, R. (1988). *Schulze Waxed Containers, Inc.* Boston, MA: Harvard Business School Publishing Case, No: 9-188-134, 1–22.

Berry, L. L., & Yadav, M. S. (1996). Capture and communicate value. *Sloan Management Review, 37*(4), 41–51.

Charnes, A., Cooper, W. W., & Rhodes, E. (1978). Measuring the efficiency of decision making units. *European Journal of Operational Research, 2*, 429–444.

Coombs M. C., & Maguire W. A. A. Toulette's Stores Ltd: A case study (unpublished, used in seminars for Argenti Southern Africa C.C.).

Cooper, R., & Kaplan, R. S. (1999). *The design of cost management systems: Text and cases* (2nd ed.). Englewood Cliffs, NJ: Prentice-Hall.

Cooper, R., & Slagmulder, R. (1997). *Target costing and value engineering.* Portland, OR: Productivity Press and IMA Foundation for Applied Research.

Cross, R. G. (1997). Launching the revenue rocket: How revenue management can work for your business. *Cornell Hotel and Restaurant Administration Quarterly, 38*, 32–43.

Disneyworld. (2010). http://www.kingdommagictravel.com/disneyworld/theme_parks/fastpass.htm (accessed August 27, 2010).

Ekelund, R. B. (1970). Price discrimination and product differentiation in economic theory: An early analysis. *The Quarterly Journal of Economics, 84*(2), 268–278.

Evans, J. R., & Berman, B. (2010). *Marketing: Marketing in the 21st century* (11th ed.). Mason, OH: Thomson.

Feller, A., Shunk, D., & Callarman, T. (2006). Value chains versus supply chains. *BPTrends* http://www.ceibs.edu/knowledge/papers/images/20060317/2847.pdf (accessed September 2010).

Fitzgerald, L., Johnston, R., Brignall, T. J., & Voss, C. (1991). *Performance measurement in service businesses.* London, England: CIMA.

Gantt, H. L. (1994, Spring). The relation between production and costs. *Cost Management,* 4–11. Reprinted from Meeting of The American Society of Mechanical Engineers, Buffalo, New York, 1915.

Goldratt, E. J., & Cox. J. (1992). *The goal* (2nd ed.). New York, NY: North River Press.

Govindarajan, V., & Shank, J. (1989, Winter). Strategic cost analysis: The Crown Cork and Seal case. *Journal of Cost Management,* 5–16.

Govindarajan, V., & Shank, J. (1992). Strategic cost management: Tailoring controls to strategies. *Journal of Cost Management, 6*(3), 14–24.

Hansen, D. R., & Mowen, M. M. (2009). *Cornerstones of cost accounting.* Mason, OH: South-Western, Cengage Learning.

Horngren, C. T., Foster, G., Datar, S. M., Rajan, M., & Ittner, C. (2009). *Cost accounting: A managerial emphasis* (13th ed.). Upper Saddle River, NJ: Pearson Prentice Hall.

Juan, C. S. (1998). *An evaluation of the activity-based model and its elements: A study of optometry services.* Business Communication (Honors) assignment. Auckland, New Zealand: Department of Accounting and Finance, The University of Auckland.

Kaplan, R. S., & Norton, D. P. (1992). The balanced scorecard-measures that drive performance. *Harvard Business Review* (January–February), 71–79.

Kaplan, R. S., & Norton, D. P. (1996). *The balanced scorecard: Translating strategy into action.* Boston, MA: Harvard Business School Press.

Kaplan, R. S., & Norton, D. P. (2001). *The strategy-focused organization: How balanced scorecard companies thrive in the new business environment.* Boston, MA: Harvard Business School Press.

Kennerley, M., & Neely, A. D. (2002). Performance measurement frameworks: A review. In A. D. Neely (Ed.), *Business performance measurement: Theory and practice* (Chapter 9). Cambridge, England: Cambridge University Press.

Kim, W. C., & Mauborgne, R. (2005). *Blue ocean strategy: How to create uncontested market space and make the competition irrelevant.* Boston, MA: Harvard Business School Press.

Kim, W. C., & Mauborgne, R. (2010). *What is blue ocean strategy? Ten key points.* http://www.blueoceanstrategy.com/abo/what_is_bos.html (accessed August 23, 2010).

Kimes, S. E. (1989). Yield management: A tool for capacity-constrained service firms. *Journal of Operations Management, 8*(4), 348–363.

Kimes, S. E. (1999). Implementing restaurant revenue management. *Cornell Hotel and Restaurant Administration Quarterly, 40*(3), 16–21.

Lee, J. Y. (1992, September). How to make financial and non-financial data add up. *Journal of Accountancy* (September), 62–66.

Littlewood, K. (1972). Forecasting and control of passengers. *12th AGIFORS Symposium Proceedings*, 95–128.

Maguire, W., & Cai, L. (2003). *Capacity management and costing in a service sector organization facing fluctuating demand.* Working paper. Auckland, New Zealand: Department of Accounting & Finance, University of Auckland.

Maguire, W., & Heath, D. (1997). Capacity management for continuous improvement. *Journal of Cost Management, 11*(1), 26–31.

Maguire, W., & Rouse, P. (1994). *Coatings New Zealand Limited.* Working paper. Auckland, New Zealand: Department of Accounting & Finance, The University of Auckland.

Maguire, W., & Rouse, P. (2004). Managing revenue to enhance profitability in service sector organizations. *Chartered Accountants Journal, 83*(5), 61–65.

Merchant, K. A., & Van der Stede, W. A. (2007). *Management control systems: Performance measurement, evaluation and incentives* (2nd ed.). Harlow, England: Financial Times/Prentice Hall.

Miles, R. E., & Snow, C. C. (1978). *Organizational strategy, structure and process.* New York, NY: McGraw-Hill.

Ng, I. C. L. (2010). The future of pricing and revenue models. *Journal of Revenue and Pricing Management, 9*(3), 276–281.

OECD (2005). *Enhancing the performance of the services sector.* Paris, France: OECD Publishing.

Pilat, D. (2005, May). Services: A sleeping giant. *OECD Observer, 24*, 917–919.

Porter, M. E. (1980). *Competitive strategy: Techniques for analyzing industries and competitors.* New York, NY: Free Press.

Porter, M. E. (1985). *Competitive advantage: Creating and sustaining superior performance.* New York, NY: Free Press.

Porter, M. E. (1998). *Competitive strategy: Techniques for analyzing industries and competitors. With a new introduction.* New York, NY: Free Press.

Porter, M. E. (2008). The five competitive forces that shape strategy. *Harvard Business Review, 86*(1), 78–93.

Prahalad, C. K., & Hamel, G. (1990). The core competence of the corporation. *Harvard Business Review, 68*(3), 79–93.

Raffish, N., & Turney, P. B. B. (1991). Glossary of activity-based management. *Journal of Cost Management, 5*(3), 53–63.

Ramsay, Gordon. http://www.gordonramsay.com/ (accessed August 27 2010).

Rosencrance, Linda. "Customers balk at variable DVD pricing." *Computerworld* (2000): 4. *General OneFile* (accessed August 23, 2010).

Rouse, A. P. B. (1997). A methodological framework of performance measurement with applications using Data Envelopment Analysis. PhD thesis, The University of Auckland.

Rouse P., Harrison, J., & Turner, N. (2010). Cost and performance: Complements for improvement. *Journal of Medical Systems*. DOI: 10.1007/s10916-010-9520-1

Rouse, P., & Putterill, M. (2003). An integral framework of performance measurement. *Management Decision, 41*(8), 791–805.

Rouse, P., & Swales, R. The search conference: A case study of a reprographics firm. Working paper. Department of Accounting and Finance, The University of Auckland.

Satariano, A. (2010, May 20). "Pricing baseball tickets like airline seats." *BusinessWeek*. http://www.businessweek.com/magazine/content/10_22/b4180039348750.htm?link_position=link5 (accessed September 2010).

Shank, J. K. (1996). "Allied Stationery" in *Cases in Cost Management*. Boston, MA: South Western College Publishing, 9–17.

Shank, J. K., & Govindarajan, V. (1989, Winter). Strategic cost management and the value chain. *Journal of Cost Management, 2*(4), 5–21.

Shank, J. K., & Govindarajan, V. (1993). What drives cost? A strategic cost management perspective. *Advances in Management Accounting, 2*, 27–46.

Stalk, G. (1992). Competing on capabilities: The new rules of corporate strategy. *Harvard Business Review, 70*(2), 57–69.

Stata, R. (1989, Spring). Organizational learning: The key to management innovation. *Sloan Management Review*, 63–74.

Steiner, G. A., Miner, J. B., & Gray, E. R. (1986). *Management Policy and Strategy*. New York, NY: Macmillan.

Teece, D. J., Pisano, G., & Shuen, A. (1997). Dynamic capabilities and strategic management. *Strategic Management Journal, 18*(7), 509–533.

Turney, P. B. B. (1992, January). Activity-based management. *Management Accounting*, 20–25.

Walczak, D., Mardan, S., & Kallesen, R. (2010). Customer choice, fare adjustments and the marginal expected revenue data transformation: A note on using old yield management techniques in the brave new world of pricing. *Journal of Revenue and Pricing Management, 9*, 94–109.

Weatherford, L. R., & Bodily, S. E. (1992). A taxonomy and research overview of perishable-asset revenue management: Yield management, overbooking, and pricing. *Operations Research, 40*(5), 831–844.

Weiss, R. M., & Mehrota, A. K. (2001, Summer). Online Dynamic Pricing: Efficiency, Equity and the Future of E-commerce. *Virginia Journal of Law and Technology*, 6.

Index

R

OTHER TITLES IN OUR MANAGERIAL ACCOUNTING COLLECTION

Series Editors: Kenneth A. Merchant

Breakeven Analysis: The Definitive Guide to Cost-Volume Profit Analysis by Michael Cafferky and Jon Wentworth

Business Planning and Entrepreneurship: An Accounting Approach by Michael Kraten

The Small Business Controller by Richard Hanson

Corporate Investment Decisions: Principles and Practice by Michael Pogue

Sustainability Reporting by Gwen White

Performance Measurement by Ken Merchant and Andy Neely

Drivers of Successful Controllership: Activities, People and Connecting with Management by Juergen Weber and Pascal Nevries

Setting Performance Targets by Carolyn Stringer and Paul Pillai

Revenue Management by Ronald J. Huefner

Working Capital Management: Principles and Practices by Michael Pogue

Cost Management and Control in Government: Leadership Driven Management's Role in Fighting the Cost War by Dale Geiger

Strategic Cost Analysis by Roger Hussey and Audra Ong